Ethnomathematics

Hirsch-
Dubin

from session:

① & working with
Gutstein - doing ethnomath
w. deaf children (she
is very cool) found out
about my Mayan math
work from him

② Af-Am. & from Texas-phd
stud.

Back to def. of mathematics: ③ & from
(p. 17) like know. in gen'l, a response to Brandeis
the drive for survival, creating who
theories & practices. Attempts to wants to
represent reality - possibly
use this eq. in
her book.
+
(p. 20)...comparing, classifying —etc.

Azure Stewart
(805) 550-3052

4/11
Theresa
Rangel-
great flight
attend-
no to Den.

B 53

↪ ⑧

The adventure of the human species is identified with the acquisition of styles of behaviors and of knowledge to survive and transcend in the distinct environments it occupies, that is, in the acquisition of

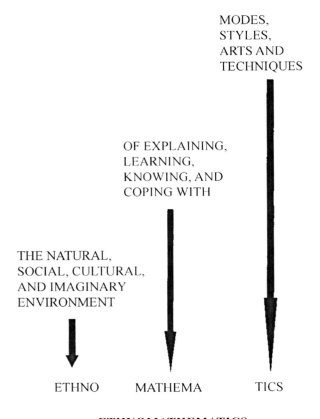

MODES, STYLES, ARTS AND TECHNIQUES

OF EXPLAINING, LEARNING, KNOWING, AND COPING WITH

THE NATURAL, SOCIAL, CULTURAL, AND IMAGINARY ENVIRONMENT

ETHNO   MATHEMA   TICS

ETHNOMATHEMATICS

Ethnomathematics
Link between Traditions and Modernity

By

Ubiratan D'Ambrosio
Unicamp, São Paulo, Brazil

SENSE PUBLISHERS
ROTTERDAM / TAIPEI

A C.I.P. record for this book is available from the Library of Congress.

ISBN 90-77874-76-3

Published by: Sense Publishers,
P.O. Box 21858, 3001 AW Rotterdam, The Netherlands
http://www.sensepublishers.com

Printed on acid-free paper

TABLE OF CONTENTS

PREFACE

Ubiratan D'Ambrosio is without a doubt the most well-known mathematics educator in Brazil, and the most well-known Brazilian mathematics educator abroad. In fact, the same could be said substituting mathematics historian, or holistic philosopher, for mathematics educator. But the key word associated with this man is ethnomathematics. Over the last thirty years, D'Ambrosio has developed this idea into a concept and a program which has inspired many researchers and educators throughout the world to emphasize listening in the classroom, and to respect social and cultural diversity. Many have come to believe, as he does, that mathematics is not solely academic mathematics, and that the "s" at the end of mathematics implies plural, meaning that mathematics can therefore have different expressions. In this book, he illustrates, in his story-telling manner, how different forms of mathematics have developed as a result of the interaction of humans with the environment. He and his followers have argued with strong support from the all the different fields they draw from − anthropology, education, history, psychology, biology, philosophy - that academic mathematics is nothing more than one expression of an incredible variety of (ethno)mathematics developed throughout different moments in history in different parts of the world.

Ubi, as many know him, has lectured in many different countries, and contributed to mathematics education in different parts of the world. He has played key roles in numerous meetings of the International Congress on Mathematics Education (ICME), which take place every four years. This conference is organized by ICMI (International Commission of Mathematics Instruction), a commission in which he has also played a key role. He has helped to broaden the notion of mathematics education by bringing the concerns and needs of developing countries to international forums. He has also played an important role in the initiation of the scientific phase of mathematics education by helping to establish graduate programs in Brazil. For example, he helped establish the first

vii

Masters program in mathematics education at UNESP, Rio Claro, São Paulo, twenty-two years ago, as well as the Doctoral program in the same institution nine years later.

D'Ambrosio was recently presented with the second Felix Klein Medal of the International Commission of Mathematics Instruction. This very important award of the mathematics education community recognizes the importance that D'Ambrosio has had for mathematics education throughout the world. In 2001, D'Ambrosio was also awarded the Kenneth O. May Medal of the International Commission of History of Mathematics/ICHM. Both, ICMI and the ICHM, are specialized commissions of the International Mathematical Union.

Although D'Ambrosio has numerous publications in various languages, this is his first book published in the English language. It is our hope that it will serve to fill a gap for mathematics educators throughout the world who have wanted to read more of his writings, but do not read Portuguese. This book was first published in Brazil in 2001 as the first in a collection of books, which now has 12 volumes, called "Trends in Mathematics Education" of which I am the coordinator. Since the book was published, it has generated, like all of D'Ambrosio's writings, considerable debate, including criticism, in the very dialogical fashion he praises so much.

With this new concept of book developed by Sense Publishers, access to his ideas will be incommensurable. Readers will be able to understand that when he mentions "Program Ethnomathematics", it is not a problem in the translation. He seeks to emphasize that a program is something more stable, developed by a collective of researchers in the same broad sense that he understands investigation in mathematics education. The study of ethnomathematics has become established; in contrast, the notion of ethnomathematics presented in this book is dynamic and does not fit in a "definition; it is in constant construction and reconstruction. That is why he explores different dimensions of ethnomathematics throughout the whole book. He presents the reader with many examples, and may entice some readers into learning Portuguese, as many of the references used for this purpose are available only in that language.

I believe the reader will find great inspiration in this book for reflection and new research. I have been Ubi's student since 1984, although I stopped studying with him formally in 1987 when he, as a member of my Masters committee, helped me in the defense of the first thesis using the notion of ethnomathematics. I continue to learn with his new ideas, but mostly with his young spirit! I am sure that the reader will share with me this experience of being his eternal student.

Marcelo C. Borba
Rio Claro, São Paulo, Brazil
April, 2006

TRANSLATOR'S ACKNOWLEDGEMENT

Although Anne Kepple is responsible for the translation, we would like to thank Arthur Powell, of Rutgers University, USA, for his helpful comments on parts of the translation, as well as the author, Ubiratan D'Ambrosio, for reviewing the entire English translation and contributing in a valuable way to the challenging task of translating his ideas into English.

INTRODUCTION

In this book, I seek to provide a general overview of ethnomathematics, focusing on the theoretical aspects.

Ethnomathematics is today considered a sub-field of the History of Mathematics and Mathematics Education, with a very natural relation to Anthropology and Cognitive Sciences. The political dimension of ethnomathematics is evident.

Ethnomathematics is the mathematics practiced by cultural groups, such as urban and rural communities, groups of workers, professional classes, children in a given age group, indigenous societies, and so many other groups that are identified by the objectives and traditions common to these groups.

In addition to this anthropological character, ethnomathematics has an undeniable political focus. Ethnomathematics is imbedded in ethics, focused on the recovery of the cultural dignity of the human being.

The dignity of the individual is violated by social exclusion, which often occurs as a result of failing to pass the discriminatory barriers established by the dominant society, including, and principally, in the school system; but also by making costumes of the traditional garb of marginalized peoples; folklore of their myths and religions; crimes of their medical practices; and for making of their traditional practices and their mathematics, mere curiosity, when not the target of derision.

In subordinating the disciplines, and scientific knowledge itself, to the greater objective of prioritizing the human being and his dignity as a cultural entity, ethnomathematics, and ethnosciences in general, and multicultural education, have been the object of criticism; by some, due to a lack of understanding, and by others, as a perverse protectionism. For these, the great goal is to maintain the status quo, covering up with the deceptive discourse of more-of-the-same [sameness] with quality.

In a way, this book continues to build on the ideas expressed in my book *Etnomatemática. Arte ou técnica de explicar e conhecer*, Editora Ática, São Paulo, 1990. Many of my more recent works in

1

check this

the field can be found on my Web site http://sites.uol.com.br/ vello/ubi.htm.

Studies in ethnomathematics have been intensifying for nearly fifteen years, when the *International Study Group of Ethnomathematics/ISGEm* was founded. With broad international participation, the ISGEm has encouraged, recognized, and publicized research in ethnomathematics. The *ISGEm Newsletter* has been published bi-annually, in English and Spanish, since August, 1995, under the responsibility of Patrick J. Scott and, since 2000, by Daniel Ness and Daniel Orey. The collection of the first thirteen years of publication, 26 issues, reunited as a compendium, constitutes a broader vision of what is available to us with respect to this new field of research. There we find reviews of studies and books, research reports, news of events, methodological suggestions, ultimately, everything necessary to be integrated into the field. The newsletters, in English and Spanish, and other information are available at http://www.rpi.edu/~eglash/isgem.htm.

Various Ethnomathematics events have taken place. In addition to the regular sessions held at the *International Congress of History of Science*, which meets every four years, the *International Congress of Mathematics Education*, which also meets every fours years, and the annual meetings of the *National Council of Teachers of Mathematics*, in the United States, the following conferences have also been held: the First International Ethnomathematics Congress in Granada, Spain, in 1998, and the second in Ouro Preto, Brazil, in 2002; the First Bolivian Congress in Ethnomathematics in Santa Cruz, Bolivia, in 1999; and the First Brazilian Congress in Ethnomathematics in São Paulo, in 2000. The proceedings of these three congresses have already been published.

Numerous theses and dissertations have been defended in universities in various countries, including Brazil, with ethnomathematics as the central theme. Also, the prestigious journal, *The Chronicle of Higher Education*, opened a debate on ethnomathematics on its site: http://chronicle.com/colloquy/2000/ ethnomath/ethnomath.htm

All this justifies considering ethnomathematics as a new field of research on the international academic scene. We are not dealing with a passing fad.

I will not be presenting a "state of the art" of ethnomathematics. In addition to the *ISGEm Newsletter* mentioned above, I recommend a collection of writings that shows the most relevant work being

2

done in ethnomathematics throughout the world: *Ethnomathematics. Challenging Eurocentrism in Mathematics Education*, eds. Arthur B. Powell and Marilyn Frankenstein, SUNY Press, Albany, 1997. In this book, Paulus Gerdes wrote a *Survey of Current Work in Ethnomathematics*, which presents a state of the art up to 1997.

Equally relevant, with a focus on history, is the book *Mathematics Across Cultures. The History of Non-Western Mathematics*, ed. Helaine Selin, Kluwer Academic Publishers, Dordrecht, 2000.

There are various publications in Portuguese, including theses and dissertations, about ethnomathematics. Some are listed in the Appendix, and some are referred to in the footnotes to the chapters.

CHAPTER 1

WHY ETHNOMATHEMATICS?

ANTECEDENTS

The voyages of the great explorers synthesized non-academic knowledge in 15th Century Europe. Although it is recognized that Portuguese universities participated in the enterprise of discovery, these discoveries surprised the Renaissance thinkers in universities and academies of other European countries to a certain extent. Mathematical knowledge of the time, which was fundamental to the discoveries, cannot be identified as a body of knowledge. It is found in various directions, in societal groups with distinct objectives.[1]

Although the first great voyages and the feat of circumnavigating the globe pertained to Spain and Portugal (Christopher Columbus, 1492; Vasco da Gama, 1498; Pedro Álvares Cabral, 1500; and Fernando de Magalhães, 1520), soon other European nations recognized the economic and political possibilities of expansion, and a new vision of the world was incorporated in the academic environment in Europe, contributing decisively to modern science.

There was surprise and curiosity throughout Europe regarding the new lands and new peoples. The discoveries, above all, of the American continent, the New World, captured the imagination of the Europeans. The Old World, Eurasia, and Africa, were familiar, as the cultural and economic exchanges recognized by historians of Antiquity date back thousands of years. Thus, these peoples and lands provoked less controversy. The new was to be found in the New World.

Spanish and Portuguese chroniclers are responsible for important literature describing the nature, phenomena, and peoples found there. Reports of other ways of thinking encountered in the lands visited are vast, always emphasizing the exotic, the curious. Particularly interesting is how the other, the new man, is viewed in the literature. One example is Shakespeare's *The Tempest*.[2]

However, recognition of other ways of thinking as systems of knowledge is belated in Europe. At the peak of colonialism, there is a great interest on the part of the European nations to come to know the peoples and lands of the planet. Great scientific expeditions emerge. In the 18th and 19th Centuries, controversy unfolds regarding the "inferiority" of the inhabitants, the fauna and flora, and the geology itself, of the New World.[3]

Of the great scientific expeditions, the one that had the largest impact may have been that of Alexander Humboldt (1768–1859), who, already at an advanced age, synthesized his vision of a harmonious universe in his book *Cosmos*. Humboldt is explicit in his adherence to Eurocentric Rationalism:

> "It is to the inhabitants of a small section of the temperate zone that the rest of mankind owe the earliest revelation of an intimate and rational acquaintance with the forces governing the physical world. Moreover, it is from the same zone (which is apparently more favorable to *the progress of reason, the softening of manners, and the security of public liberty*) that the germs of civilization have been carried to the regions of the tropics (italics mine)."[4]

The phrase emphasized above reveals the acceptance of the "incivility" found in the New World as being intrinsic to the New World, thus justifying a civilizing mission of the immigrant. We shall not forget that *Cosmos* was a best-seller, widely translated throughout Europe. The immigrant arriving with a mission to civilize could rarely recognize the local culture, a mixture of the cultures of the first colonizers with the cultures of the indigenous people and the Africans who were brought as slaves. It is enough to observe that the most widely spoken language in Brazil when the Royal family arrived was a variation of Tupi. The opinion that there lacked capacity to organize a political system has much to do with the political framework that was implanted in the Americas following independence. The essential difference of the independence of the United States compared to other countries of the New World is a fundamental question pointed out by the historian Herbert Aptheker when he said that the American revolution was, in fact, an English revolution that took place on the other side of the Atlantic. The characteristics of the formation of American nations following their independence varied greatly.

Returning to Humboldt, he does not fail to recognize that there is something fundamental that differentiates the knowledge and behavior of the rest of the other peoples of the planet from those that have their origin in the Mediterranean civilizations. In *Cosmos* one reads:

"We find even among the most savage nations (as my own travels enable me to attest) a certain vague, terror-stricken sense of the all-powerful unity of natural forces, and of the existence of an invisible, spiritual essence manifested in these forces, whether in unfolding the flower and maturing the fruit of the nutrient tree, in upheaving the soil of the forest, or in rending the clouds with the might of the storms. We may here trace the revelation of a bond of union, linking together the visible world and that higher spiritual world which escapes the grasp of the senses. The two become unconsciously blended together, developing in the mind of man, as a simple product of ideal conception, and independently of the aid of observation, the first germ of a Philosophy of Nature." [5]

Soon after the end of World War I, a German philosopher, Oswald Spengler (1880-1936) proposed a philosophy of history that sought to understand the West through a new lens, viewing culture as an organic whole. The book *The Decadence of the West. Form and Reality,* published in 1918, was soon followed by a second volume, *The Decadence of the West. Perspectives of the Universal History*, published in 1922. The books were taken out of circulation in 1933. This book, which has an encyclopedic character, opened up new possibilities for understanding the nature of mathematical thought. Spengler wrote:

From this follows a decisive circumstance which, until now, has escaped mathematicians themselves. If mathematics were a mere science, like astronomy or mineralogy, it would be possible to define its object. There is, however, no single mathematics; there are many mathematics. What we call "the" history of mathematics − a supposed progressive approximation to a single, immutable ideal − becomes, in reality, once the deceiving image of the surface of history is dismissed, a plurality of independent processes, complete in themselves; a sequence of births of worlds of forms, new and distinct, that are incorporated, transformed, abolished; a purely organic florescence, of fixed duration, followed by phases of maturity, of decay, of death. [6]

Spengler seeks to understand mathematics as a living cultural manifestation, going so far as to say that the Gothic cathedrals and Doric temples are petrified mathematics. Spengler declares himself to be an admirer of the thinking of Goethe, who was criticized by Humboldt, and sees mathematics as totally integrated with the other manifestations of a culture.[7]

Although he refers exclusively to the West, Spengler's ideas serve to encourage the examination of the mathematics of other cultures.

The 20th Century sees the emergence of anthropology and much attention given to understanding the ways of thinking of other cultures. However, perhaps the first explicit recognition of other systems of rationalization and their pedagogical implications is owed to the noted Japanese algebrist, Yasuo Akizuki, in 1960:

> I can, therefore, imagine that other modes of thinking can also exist, even in mathematics. Thus, I think that we should not limit ourselves to directly applying the methods that are currently considered as the best in Europe and America, but should study the mathematical instruction appropriate for Asia.[8]

The recognition, albeit belated, of other ways of thinking, including mathematical, encourages broader reflections about the nature of mathematical thought, from the cognitive, historical, social and pedagogical points of view. This is the objective of the Ethnomathematics Program.

THE PROGRAM ETHNOMATHEMATICS

The great motivator for the research program known as Ethnomathematics is to seek to understand mathematical knowing/doing throughout the history of humanity, in the contexts of different interest groups, communities, peoples and nations. This denomination will be justified throughout this book.

Why do I talk about Ethnomathematics as a research program and, at the same time, often use the term Program Ethnomathematics?

The principle reason results from my concern regarding attempts to propose an epistemology, and as such, an explanation for Ethnomathematics. Upon insisting on the name Program Ethnomathematics, I seek to make evident that the intention is not to propose another epistemology, but rather to understand the adventure of the human species in the search for knowledge and the adoption of behaviors.

The critics of the epistemological proposals that polarized the philosophy of science in the 1970's around Popper and Kuhn, and that placed Lakatos and Feyerabend in oddly opposed camps, had an influence on my interest in ethnomathematics. I see the denomination Program Ethnomathematics as being at the same time more in line with the posture of permanent seeking, proposed by transdisciplinarity, and more immune to the attacks from both sides that are sparring in the so-called "science wars".[9]

Research in ethnomathematics should be done with much rigor, but the subordination of this rigor to a language and a standard methodology, even with an interdisciplinary character, can be deleterious to the Program Ethnomathematics.[10] In recognizing that it is not possible to arrive at a final theory of the ways of knowing/doing mathematics of a culture, I want to emphasize the dynamic character of this research program. I highlight the fact that we need to always be open to new foci, new methodologies, and new views of what science is and how it evolves, which results in a dynamic historiography.[11]

Every living person develops knowledge and has behavior that reflects this knowledge, which in turn becomes modified as a function of the results of the behavior. For every individual, her behavior and knowledge are in permanent transformation, and relate to each other in a truly symbiotic way, in total inter-dependence.

THE NOTION OF CULTURE

The drive for survival, of the individual and of the species, which characterizes life, manifests itself when the individual turns to nature for survival and seeks and finds the other, of the same species, albeit biologically different (male/female) to continue the species.

The human species also obeys this instinct. Individuals seek and find others, exchange knowledge and behaviors, and common interests, which are communicated between them, keeping them in association and in societies, organized at various levels: groups of common interests, families, tribes, communities, nations.

The everyday life of groups, families, tribes, communities, associations, professions, and nations takes place in different regions of the planet, in different ways and at different paces, as the result of certain priorities, among many factors, due to environmental conditions, models of urbanization and production, systems of communication, and power structures.

Upon recognizing that the individuals of a nation, community, or group share their knowledge, such as language, systems of explanation, myths and spiritual gatherings, customs and culinary habits, and that their behaviors are made compatible with and subordinated to value systems agreed to by the group, we say that these individuals pertain to a culture. In sharing knowledge and making behavior compatible, the characteristics of a culture are synthesized. Thus we speak of the culture of the family, the tribe, the community, the association, the profession, the nation.

A dynamic of interaction that is always present in the encounter of individuals makes it impossible to speak with precision about cultures, final or extant. Cultures are in incessant transformation, obeying what we could call a cultural dynamic.[12]

The distinct ways of doing (practice) and knowing (theory) that characterize a culture are part of the shared knowledge and the behavior that has become compatible. Like behavior and knowledge, the ways of knowing and doing are in permanent interaction. The dichotomies between knowing and doing are false, as are those between theory and practice.

NOURISHMENT, SPACE, AND TIME

The need to eat, in competition with other species, is the great stimulus for the development of instruments to help obtain food. Thus, there is evidence of instruments made of carved stone that, close to two million years ago, were used to carve meat, thus improving the quality and quantity of food available. Of course the stone carved with this objective must have the appropriate dimensions to accomplish this end. The evaluation of the appropriate dimensions for carved stone may be the first mathematical manifestation of the species. Fire, which became widely used some 500,000 years ago, even lends characteristics of social organization to food provisioning.[13]

From the use of dead animal carcasses, humans began killing live prey. The invention of the lance brought greater security to man for killing prey, which were generally larger and stronger than he was. Wooden lances, of approximately 2.5 meters, appeared around

10

250,000 years ago. Man's use of the lance, his muscular coordination, perception of target, and recognition of vulnerable parts of the prey, demonstrate the development of a great capacity for observation and analysis.

The circumstantial and occasional slaughter of prey obviously had an irregular character in the social organization. However, upon creating the possibility of slaughtering herds, the organization of hunting groups became necessary, with a hierarchical structure and leadership, distribution of functions, and organization of space. The social life thus became much more complex. The learning of habits and behaviors by the species, not only by individuals, shows the development of the capacity to classify objects (individuals) according to specific qualities.

This was a decisive step, recognized as occurring around 40,000 years ago, in the evolution of the human species, giving origin to the organization of the first societies. The cooperation between groups of relatively numerous individuals, centered on myths and symbolic representations, was probably responsible for the emergence of song [**time**] and dance [**space**], which led groups of individuals to form distinct families to be together, their symbolic universe situated in time and space. According to William H. McNeill, song and dance were the first great innovation distinguishing the evolutionary course of humans from their closest relatives, the chimpanzees.[14] Dance and song are intimately associated with mathematical representations of time and space. From the meeting of these larger groups, it is probable that language evolved, such as articulated speech and grammar.

All these inventions presaged agriculture, which developed around 10,000 years ago, and was the most important conceptual transition in the history of humanity. Agriculture made possible patterns of subsistence that could not possibly be achieved by groups of hunters and gatherers. The human species encountered, thanks to agriculture, its best manner of food provisioning.[15]

The emergence of agriculture represented, especially among civilizations around the Mediterranean, a conceptual transition from a matriarchal to a patriarchal vision of the world. Up until the invention of agriculture, the great divinities were feminine. It was with the emergence of agriculture that a god identified as masculine manifested itself.[16]

The populations grew and the need emerged for intellectual instruments for planning planting, harvest, and storage, and consequently, organization of land occupation, organized production, and work, providing a basis for structures of power and economy that are still prevalent today. Myths and rituals linked to seasonal phenomena affecting agriculture emerged. It became important to know where [**space**] and when [**time**] to plant, harvest, and store.

Geometry [*geo*=land, *metry*=measure] is the result of the pharaohs' practice that made it possible to feed the population in years of low productivity, distribute productive lands along the banks of the Nile River, and measure them following floods to collect the part destined for storage, a form of taxation.[17]

Calendars synthesize the knowledge and behaviors necessary for the success of the stages of planting, harvest, and storage, and are obviously associated with the myths and rituals directed at the entities responsible for this success, which guaranteed the survival of the community. Therefore, calendars were local.

Although the internationally recognized calendar was the one proclaimed by Pope Gregorio XIII, in effect since October 15, 1582, there are around forty calendars currently in use today. The construction of calendars, i.e., the counting and recording of time, is an excellent example of ethnomathematics.[18]

Many may find it strange that I give so much emphasis to understanding food provisioning and issues of agriculture. Without a doubt, food provisioning, nourishment for survival, was always the main necessity before all others for all living things. With the emergence of agriculture, the first organized societies begin to be identified. Geo-metry and calendars are examples of an ethnomathematics associated with a system of production, in response to the principle need of organized societies to feed their people.

Knowledge and behaviors are shared and made compatible, making the continuation of these societies possible. This knowledge and these behaviors are recorded, orally or graphically, and disseminated and passed from generation to generation. Thus is born the history of groups, families, tribes, communities, and nations.

This has great importance in education. A mathematics project centered on the construction of home gardens, developed by José Carlos Borsato, is among the first ethnomathematics projects oriented toward pedagogical practice. At that time, the term ethnomathematics was not in use.[19]

More recently, the work of Gelsa Knijnik[20] and Alexandrina Monteiro,[21] among many others, focuses on ethnomathematics developed and practiced by families involved in organized actions to occupy unused farmland. These actions are, in Brazil, organized as the *Movimento dos Sem Terra/MST*.

MATHEMATICS IN EVERYDAY LIFE

Among the different ways of doing and knowing, some privilege comparing, classifying, quantifying, measuring, explaining, generalizing, inferring, and, in some way, evaluating. We are then talking of a knowing/doing mathematics that seeks explanations and ways of dealing with the immediate and remote environment. Obviously, this knowing/doing mathematics is contextualized and responds to natural and social factors.

Everyday life is impregnated in the knowledge and practices of a culture. At all times, individuals are comparing, classifying, quantifying, measuring, explaining, generalizing, inferring, and, in some way, evaluating, using material and intellectual instruments that belong to their culture.

There are innumerable studies about the ethnomathematics present in everyday life. It is an ethnomathematics that is not learned in school, but rather in the family environment, the environment of toys and work, received from friends and colleagues. How does this learning take place? Maria Luisa Oliveras, working with artisans in Granada, Spain, identified what she called ethno-didactics.[22]

We recognize the practical mathematics of market vendors. The pioneering research of Terezinha Nunes, David Carraher, and Ana Lúcia Schliemann recognized how children helping their parents in open-air markets in Recife, Brazil, acquire very sophisticated arithmetic practices to deal with money, make change, and offer discounts while still making a profit.[23]

The use of day-to-day shopping to teach mathematics reveals practices learned outside the school environment, a true ethnomathematics of commerce. An important component of ethnomathematics is making a critical view of reality possible using instruments of a mathematical nature. Comparative analysis of prices, bills, budgets, provides excellent pedagogical material. The work of Marilyn Frankenstein in the U.S.A. is pioneering in proposing critical mathematics in the schools.[24] A similar proposal,

13

using products found in supermarkets as a reference, was developed in Italy by Cinzia Bonotto.[25]

Seeking to perceive the influence that the parents' profession has on their children's achievement in school, Adriana M. Marafon identified mathematical practices of mechanics who repair and change tires.[26]

Groups of professionals practice their own ethnomathematics. Observing numerous surgical operations, Tod L. Shockey identified, in his doctoral dissertation, mathematical practices of heart surgeons, focusing on criteria for making decisions about time and risk, and topological notions in the manipulation of the suture knots.[27] Maria de Carmo Villa researched the manner in which fruit juice vendors decide, using a probability model, the quantity of each fruit juice that they should have available in their juice stand to satisfactorily meet the demands of their customers.[28] N.M. Acioly and Sergio R. Nobre identified the mathematics practiced by *bicheiros*, illegal betting ticket vendors, to practice an attractive and compensatory scheme of bets.[29] The mathematics of the *jogo de bicho*, a widely-practiced illegal betting game, had already attracted the interest of Malba Tahan.[30] Marcelo de Carvalho Borba analyzed the way children living in a poor neighborhood organized to build a soccer field, obeying the official dimensions in scale.[31]

The recognition of mathematical practices in everyday life in Africa has been the object of important studies.[32] A very interesting example is the use of percussion instruments, an integral part of traditions originating in Africa. The rhythm that accompanies the percussion instruments can be studied to aid the understanding of ratios.[33]

The work of Claudia Zaslavsky deserves special mention. Her pioneering book, published in 1973, recognized that many of the mathematical practices found in Africa have characteristics of their own, a true ethnomathematics, although the term was not yet in use at that time.[34]

The interest in the ethnomathematics of African cultures has grown tremendously. The work of Paulus Gerdes and collaborators in Mozambique deserves to be highlighted, with publications in Portuguese and English, studying largely traditional basket weaving, textiles, and games of southern Africa.[35]

In the Americas, ethnomathematics appears strongly in the remaining native cultures. There is a great interest in historical study of the mathematics existing during the arrival of the conquistadors

14

and practiced during the colonial period[36]; however, descendents of native cultures continue to practice their ethnomathematics.

Conciliating the need to teach the dominant mathematics and, at the same time, give recognition to the ethnomathematics of their traditions, is the great challenge for education for indigenous peoples. This theme was discussed by Samuel López Bello, working together with teachers from the Quechua tradition in Bolivia.[37]

Economic relations and systems of production are important factors in the development and transformation of ethnomathematics as a body of knowledge, as Chateaubriand Nunes Amâncio showed.[38]

The vast bibliography available today makes it impossible, in one short book, to attempt a type of "State of the Art" of research in ethnomathematics. In fact, this is not the intention of this publication. However it is justifiable to give some guidance to those who wish to delve deeper into ethnomathematics, from the point of view of research as well as pedagogy.

A special volume of *Teaching Children Mathematics,* a periodical of the National Council of Mathematics Teachers, focused on *"Mathematics and culture"*. It is a collection of various studies, all focused on the school.

As I sought to demonstrate in this chapter, ethnomathematics is part of everyday life, which is the universe in which the expectations and anxieties of children and adults are situated.

CHAPTER 2

THE VARIOUS DIMENSIONS OF ETHNOMATHEMATICS

THE CONCEPTUAL DIMENSION

Ethnomathematics is a research program about the history and philosophy of mathematics, with obvious implications for teaching.

I shall begin with a reflection on the origin of mathematical ideas. How did mathematics come to be?

Mathematics, like knowledge in general, is a response to the drive for survival and transcendence, which synthesize the existential question of the human species. The species creates theories and practices that resolve the existential question. These theories and practices are based on the elaboration of knowledge, and decisions regarding behavior, based on representations of reality. The representations respond to the perception of space and time. The virtuality of these representations, which is manifested in the elaboration of models, distinguishes the human species from other animal species.

For all living species, the question of survival is resolved by behaviors of immediate response, here and now, elaborated on the real, and falling back on the previous experiences [knowledge] of the individual and the species [incorporated into the genetic code]. Behavior is based on knowledge and, at the same time, produces new knowledge. This symbiosis of behavior and knowledge is what we refer to as instinct, which resolves the question of survival of the individual and the species.

In the human species, the question of survival is accompanied by that of transcendence: the "here and now" is broadened to include the "where" and "when". The human species transcends space and time to go beyond the immediate and the perceivable. The present is prolonged by the past and the future, and the perceivable is broadened to include the remote. The human being acts as a function of his sensorial capacity, which responds to the material [artifacts], and of his imagination, often called creativity, which responds to the abstract [mentifacts].

17

The material reality is the accumulation of facts and phenomena accumulated from the beginning. What is the beginning, in space and time? That is the greatest question of all religious, philosophical, and scientific systems.

The reality perceived by each individual of the human species is the natural reality, together with the total of artifacts and mentifacts [experiences and ways of thinking] accumulated by him and by the species [culture]. This reality, through genetic and sensorial mechanisms and memory [knowledge] inform each individual. Each individual processes this information, which defines their action, resulting in their behavior and the generation of more knowledge. The accumulation of knowledge shared by the individuals of a group has the consequence of making the behavior of these individuals compatible, and, accumulated, this shared knowledge and "compatibilized" behavior constitute the culture of the group.

THE HISTORICAL DIMENSION

We live at the moment of apogee of modern science, which is a system of knowledge that originated in the Mediterranean basin nearly 3,000 years ago, and which imposed itself on the whole planet. This rapid evolution is a short period in the entire history of humanity, and there is no indication that it will be permanent. What will come afterwards? Without a doubt, as has always happened with other systems of knowledge, modern science itself will develop the intellectual instruments to criticize itself and to incorporate elements of other systems of knowledge.

These intellectual instruments depend strongly on a historical interpretation of the knowledge of the Egyptians, Babylonians, Jews, Greeks, and Romans, from which modern knowledge originated.

Throughout nearly three millennia, transitions between the qualitative and the quantitative can be noted in the analysis of facts and phenomena. What could be called the quantitative reasoning of the Babylonians gave way to the qualitative reasoning characteristic of the Greeks, which prevailed throughout the entire Middle Ages.

Modernity came about with the incorporation of quantitative reasoning, made possible thanks to arithmetic [*tica*=art + *aritmos*=numbers], done with Indo-Arabic algorithms, and later, with the extensions of Simon Stevin [decimals] and John Neper [logarithms], culminating with computers. In this evolution, quantitative reasoning, which can be considered the essence of modernity, was privileged. More recently, we see an intense search for qualitative reasoning, particularly through artificial intelligence. This trend is in step with the intensification of interest in ethnomathematics, whose qualitative character is strongly predominant.

Another aspect of the evolution of Western thought that should be noted is the subordination of global thought, such as predominated in the southern Mediterranean cultures, by sequential thought, which came to characterize Greek philosophy. This culminated in the thought of René Descartes, resulting in the organization of disciplines, which prevailed over the holistic proposals of Jan Comenius.

We are now living in a time which resembles the intellectual effervescence of the Middle Ages. It is thus justifiable to speak of a new renaissance. Ethnomathematics is one of the manifestations of this new renaissance.

It is important to note that the acceptance and incorporation of other ways of analyzing and explaining facts and phenomena, as in the case of ethnomathematics, always occurs in parallel with other manifestations of culture. This is evident in the two attempts to introduce the Indo-Arabic system in Europe. The first attempt, by Gerbert de Aurillac, who was ordained as Pope Silvester II in 999, was unsuccessful.[1] The second attempt, almost three centuries later, was promoted by the merchant Leonardo Fibonacci, of Pisa, with the publication *Liber Abaci*, in 1202. The new system taught by Sylvester II contributed little for the economic model and technology that prevailed in the 11th Century. However, for the merchant trade that began to develop in the 13th Century, as well as for the advances in experimental science in the late Middle Ages, the arithmetic learned from the Arabs was essential.

This parallel between mathematical ideas and economic models was recognized by Frei Vicente de Salvador when he commented on the arithmetic of the indigenous Brazilians. The historian explained that they counted with their fingers and, if necessary their toes. With this, all of their day-to-day needs [of survival] and for their systems of explanation [of transcendence] were perfectly satisfied. They knew no other systems because their was no reason to.[2] Today, native Brazilians want calculators because they are essential for their commercial relations.

It would not be possible to understand the behavior of today's youth and, thus, evaluate the state of education, without turning to an analysis of the cultural moment in which youth are living. This leads us to an examination of what is happening with the central discipline of the curricula, which is mathematics; not only in the discipline itself, which necessarily leads us to intercultural reflections on the history and philosophy of mathematics, but just as importantly, on how mathematics is situated today in the individual and collective experience of each individual.

THE COGNITIVE DIMENSION

Mathematical ideas, in particular, comparing, classifying, quantifying, measuring, explaining, generalizing, inferring, and to an extent, evaluating, are forms of thinking present in the entire human species. The attention of scientists who study cognition has been increasingly directed to this characteristic of the species.

The emergence of mathematical thinking in individuals, and in the human species as a whole, has been the subject of intense research. Much is already known about the brain, and we know much about cranial matter. It has even been attempted to privilege brain lobes with specific actions! But where is the capacity to prefer one color over another, and the reason why a smell awakens emotions? There is a fundamental difference between the mind and the brain. The new science of cognition has received great contributions from neurologists. [3]

The attention of researchers is focused on studies of the mind, or of consciousness. Many call this field of science the frontier of science. What is thinking? What is consciousness? Studies of the mind or of consciousness, common among neurologists, including neurosurgeons, have attracted the growing attention of mathematicians and theoretical physicists. [4]

In order to understand humans, it is, of course, important to know about those living beings that have some similarity with humans, in particular, the primates. It is enough to note that 98% of the genome of the *rhesus*, is identical to humans. Primates have been the subject of considerable research. The emergence of thinking of a mathematical nature, privileging the quantitative, has been noted in primates. [5]

20

It is equally important to create automated devices and models that, at least partially, carry out functions similar to those performed by humans. Without a doubt, calculators and computers have proven efficient for tasks involving quantification. But the greatest challenge is qualitative thinking, which includes emotions. This lies within the sphere of robotics and artificial intelligence. One fascinating theme is the study of autonomous "mental" development in robots, as a result of experiences with the natural environment.[6]

But let us return to our species, where the ideas of comparing, classifying, quantifying, measuring, explaining, generalizing, inferring, and to an extent, evaluating, appear as characteristics.

The species *Homo sapiens sapiens* is new, having been identified approximately 40 thousand years ago. The species that preceded it, the Australopithecus, appeared nearly 5 million years ago, close to what is known today as Tanzania, and spread over the planet. In this expansion, the species underwent transformation, influenced by the climate, food habits, and various other factors, and developed techniques and abilities that allowed their survival in the new regions they encountered. When confronted with new situations, we gather experiences from previous situations, adapting them to new circumstances, thus incorporating to the memory new ways of knowing and doing. Thanks to an elaborate system of communication, the ways and modes of dealing with situations are shared, transmitted, and disseminated.

Although knowledge is generated individually, from information received from reality, perhaps one of the characteristics that most distinguishes the human species from other species is the phenomenon of communication, which takes place in the encounter with the other. Through communication, the information received by one individual is enriched by the information received by another. The knowledge generated by the individual, which is a result of processing the totality of information available, is, also through communication, shared, at least partially, with the other. This is extended, obviously, to others and to the group. Thus, the knowledge shared by the group is developed.

The behavior of each individual, associated with her knowledge, is modified by the presence of the other, largely by the knowledge of the consequences for the other. This is reciprocal, and thus, the behavior of one individual is made compatible with the behavior of the other. Obviously, this extends to the others and to the group. Thus, the *compatibilized* behavior of the group is developed.

Culture is the set of shared knowledge and *compatiblized* behavior.

As I already mentioned in the introduction, we have evidence of a species, a type of Australopithecus, that lived about 2.5 million years ago and used instruments made of chiseled stone to clean animal carcasses. It is easy to understand that, when eating a slaughtered animal, the existence of an instrument such as a chiseled stone would make it possible to scrape the bone, and thus, not only make use of every piece of meat, but also extract nutrients from the bone that would not otherwise be available using the teeth alone. The species began to have more food of higher nutritional value. This appears to have been a decisive factor in the refinement of the brain of the species that dominated this technology.

What does this have to do with ethnomathematics?

At the moment this Australopithecus selected and chiseled a piece of stone with the objective of de-boning a piece of meat, his mathematical mind revealed itself. To select the stone, one must evaluate its dimensions; and in order to chisel it as needed and sufficiently to fulfill the objectives for which it is intended, it is necessary to evaluate and compare dimensions. Evaluating and comparing dimensions is one of the most elementary manifestations of mathematical thinking. Thus, a first example of ethomathematics was that practiced by this Australopithecus.

As they evolved and spread throughout the various regions of the planet in small groups, the species that preceded us continued to refine the material and intellectual instruments needed to deal with their environment, and to develop new instruments.

In various regions of the planet, the different languages began to take form, making it possible to organize systems of knowledge. Records began to be made. Especially rich are the records of Eurasia, and a pre-history of the mathematical ideas from which academic mathematics originated. In pre-history and in history, ethnomathematics is identified as a knowledge system.[7]

Man seeks explanations for everything, and very naturally associates these explanations with what he sees but does not understand: the climate, day and night, the stars in the sky. What is occurring, what is perceived and felt at every moment, may be indicators of what is going to occur. This is the mystery. Seeking explanations for the mystery that relates causes and effects is an important step in the evolution of the *homo* species.

Systems of explanation for the first causes are organized [myths of creation]. Death, which is so evident, may not be the end, but rather an encounter with the first causes. What happens after death? An even more practical question occurs: what will happen next, in the following moment? What are the consequences of what I am seeing now? Of what I am doing now? Only whoever is responsible for the first causes [a diety] could know the mystery of what will come to pass.

How to ask the deity what will come to pass? Through the techniques of "consulting" the deity. These techniques are called divination arts. How to influence the deity so that desirable, necessary, and pleasant things happen? Through worship, sacrifice, and magic.

Religions are systems of knowledge that allow us to delve into the past - explaining the first causes, developing a sense of history and organizing traditions - and influence the future. The knowledge of these traditions is shared by the group. Continuing to belong to the group, even after death, depends on behaving, in life, in response to his shared knowledge. This knowledge, which is compatible and shared by the group, is subordinated to parameters that we call values.

THE CHALLENGES OF EVERYDAY LIFE

One of the most important things in our relationship with the environment is obtaining nutrition and protection from the elements. Knowing the environment, we can act in such a way that our ability to nourish and protect ourselves depends less on factors such as the weather.

Once they had mastered techniques of agriculture, raising livestock, and construction, humans were able to remain in the same location, to be born and die in the same place. They perceived the time needed for germination and gestation, the time that passed between planting and harvest. At a certain moment, a configuration of the sky coincided with the sprouting of the little plants. It is a divine message. It was learned how to interpret these messages, which are generally translated into periods characteristic of what are known as seasons of the year.

Insemination was more difficult to perceive, but the time from gestation to birth is more easily recognized. The regularity of the menstrual cycle, and the relationship between its interruption and gestation, have long been recognized. Recognizing and recording the menstrual cycle, associated with the phases of the moon, appear to have been among the first forms of ethnomathematics.

Agriculture had a large influence on the history of ideas of the peoples of the Mediterranean. The theories that made it possible to know the correct time for planting emerged, subordinated to tradition. Recognizing the seasons and celebrating their arrival, like an appeal and subsequent acknowledgment to the one responsible for the regularity, a deity, marked the first moments of worship and religion. The association of religion with astronomy, with agriculture, and with fertility is obvious.

Mathematics began to be organized as an instrument of analysis of the conditions of the sky and daily necessities. I could go on describing how, here and there, in all corners of the planet and at all times, mathematical ideas were being developed that were important in the creation of systems of knowledge and, consequently, behaviors necessary to deal with the environment, to survive and explain the visible and the invisible.

Culture, which is the set of *compatiblized* behaviors and shared knowledge, includes values. In the same culture, individuals provide the same explanations and use the same material and intellectual instruments in their everyday activities. The set of these instruments is manifested in the manners, modes, abilities, arts, techniques – in the *tics* of dealing with the environment, of understanding and explaining facts and phenomena, of teaching and sharing all this, which is the **mathema** of the group, of the community, of the **ethno**. That is, it is their ethnomathematics.

In different environments, the ethnomathematics are, of course, different. The Eskimos at the Arctic Circle, when seeking to feed themselves, cannot think in terms of planting, and therefore, never developed agriculture. They dedicated themselves to fishing. Hence, they needed to know the best time to fish. They must fish a lot, perhaps all day long. But the day [light] lasts six months, and the night [dark], six months. Thus, their distribution of time, and the perception they have of the heavens and the forces that influence their day-to-day lives, is quite different from those whose daily lives are spent in the Mediterranean or near the Equator. Their astronomy and their religion are distinct from those that emerged in the Mediterranean or near the Equator, as well as their ways of dealing with their everyday needs. Their ethnomathematics is different.

One of the main things that appears at the beginning of mathematical thinking are ways of counting time. In the history of mathematics (and now I am speaking of academic mathematics, which has its origins in Greece), the great names are linked to astronomy. Geometry, in its origin and in its very name, is related to measurements of land. As Herodoto tells us, geometry was learned from the Egyptians, for whom it was more than a mere measurement of land; it had everything to do with the system of taxation of productive areas. Behind this development, we see an entire system of production and an economic, social, and political structure that requires measurement of land and, at the same time, arithmetic to deal with the economy and with counting time.

While this system of knowledge was developing over 2,500 years ago in civilizations surrounding the Mediterranean, the indigenous peoples of the Amazon forest were also trying to learn about and cope with their environment, developing systems of production and social systems which, in the same way, required measurements of space and of time. The same was true of the Eskimos, the Andean civilizations, and those of China, India, and sub-Saharan Africa – of the entire planet. They were all developing their ways of knowing.

THE EPISTEMOLOGICAL DIMENSION

Knowing what? System of knowledge for what? Knowledge systems make survival possible, but they also respond to fundamental existential questions, such as: Where did I come from? Where am I going? What is my past and the past of my people? What will the future be, mine and that of my people? How to go beyond the current moment, delve into my questioning and objectives, in the past and in the future? How to transcend the here and now?

Knowledge systems are sets of responses that a group gives to its drives for survival and transcendence, inherent to the human species. How are knowledge and practices related?

25

The great controversy of the history of science is the relation between the empirical and the theoretical, which can be summarized in three direct questions:

1. How do we move from ad hoc observations and practices to experimentation and method?
2. How do we move from experimentation and method to reflection and abstraction?
3. How do we proceed toward inventions and theories?

This sequence serves as the basis for explaining the evolution of knowledge, i.e., for a theory of knowledge, or epistemology.[8]

My criticism of epistemology is that it focuses on knowledge already established, according to the accepted paradigms of the time and of the moment. But the dynamic of the generation of knowledge, of its intellectual and social development, of its diffusion and, consequently, of the returns of this knowledge to those responsible for its production, constitute an integral cycle, and attempts to study this cycle by isolating its components is inappropriate for non-Western systems of knowledge. This becomes very clear when one seeks to focus on theories for ethnomathematics. As Eglash has said, [Western] mathematics is seen as the culmination of a singular, sequential development of human thought. This perception, which he classifies as mythology, is confused with the predominant epistemologies. [9]

My proposal for an epistemology that is appropriate for understanding the cycle of knowledge in an integrated manner can be synthesized in Figure 1.

The fragmentation of this cycle is absolutely inappropriate for understanding the cycle of knowledge. The historiography associated with the fragmentation of the cycle cannot lead to an integral perception of how humanity evolved. Fragmentation is particularly inappropriate for analyzing the mathematical knowledge of peripheral cultures. [10]

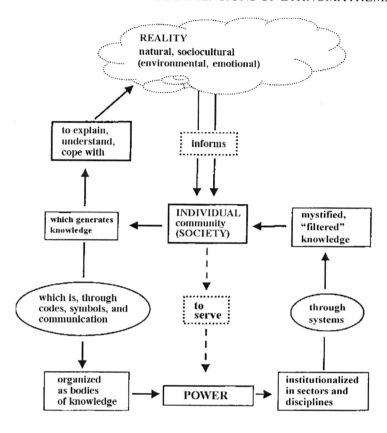

Figure 1.

THE POLITICAL DIMENSION

Nearly 2,500 years ago, a change of power emerged in the region of the Mediterranean. Egyptians and Babylonians, who had based their hegemony on the subordination of their knowledge and behavior to a broad polytheism, were challenged by the great innovation, proposed by the Jews, of a single, abstract god.

The Greeks, and soon thereafter, the Romans, polytheist pagans, expanded the domain of the Mediterranean eastward, conquering thousand-year-old civilizations, such as those of Persia and India, and toward northern Europe, conquering the barbarian peoples. Greece and Rome, which imposed their knowledge systems and social and political organization on the conquered peoples, were equally challenged by the idea of a single, abstract god, above all, by the emergent idea of Christianity.

With the adoption of Christian monotheism in the 4th Century, Rome imposed not only its politics, science, technology, and philosophy, but primarily, the new religion on a large part of Eurasia above the Tropic of Cancer.

The Roman Empire, imposing its own ways of responding to its drives for survival and transcendence, proved to be efficient in its encounters with other cultures, being successful in its conquests, religious conversion, and consequently, the expansion of its power.

The peak of this success occurred during the transition from the 15th to the 16th Centuries. In about 25 years, navigators from Spain and Portugal circumnavigated the globe. They were soon accompanied by other European nations, and by sea, traveled to the North, South, East and West, in every direction, conquering peoples and carrying with them their explanations and ways of dealing with the environment, modes and styles of production and of power. The process of globalization of the planet had begun.

When speaking of conquest, we are, of course, recognizing the existence of a conqueror and the conquered. The conqueror cannot allow the conquered to manifest themselves. The fundamental strategy in the process of conquest adopted by a [dominant] individual, group, or culture, is to maintain the other [dominated] individual, group, or culture in an inferior position. One very efficient way to keep an individual, group, or culture inferior is to weaken their roots, removing the historical ties and historicity of the dominated. This is the most effective way to carry out a conquest.

Removing the historicity implies removing the language, production, religion, authority, recognition, land and nature, and the systems of explanation in general. For example, practically any indigenous Brazilian can recite the Lord's Prayer and the Ave Maria and believes in God and in Christ, even though this entire system has nothing to do with their traditions. Upon seeing the system of production that sustains them destroyed or modified, the dominated begin to eat -and to like - what the dominator eats.

Thus, the strategies of the dominated for survival and transcendence are eliminated and substituted. In some cases, the conquered individual himself was eliminated, in an evident act of genocide.

Over a period of 300 years, not only was the culture eliminated, but the individuals of this culture, as well, as occurred with the indigenous peoples of the Atlantic Coast of the Americas and the Caribbean, who were exterminated. In other regions of the planet, many individuals survived. They remained in marginalized and excluded cultural groups, or were co-opted and assimilated into the culture of the dominator.[11]   However, a latent culture, often disguised or clandestine, maintained itself during the period of colonization.

The importation of Africans for slavery in the Americas should be given particular emphasis.   The New World underwent, and continues to undergo, great transformations in the conjunction of the indigenous, African, and European cultures.   The transfer of African cultures to the New World, and their preservation, incorporating and modifying linguistic, religious, artistic, and above all, scientific traditions, has as yet been analyzed very little by historians.[12]

A similar situation takes place in the schools.   The school has broadened its reach, taking in youth from the villages, to whom it offers the possibility of social access.   But this access occurs as a function of the results, which is one modality of co-optation. Systems for choosing who will merit access are created and justified by convenient theories of behavior and learning.   One very important instrument of selection is language.   Latin was the standard, later substituted by the cultivated norm of language.   Even today, many children feel inhibited to speak because they know they speak incorrectly and, since they are unable to speak correctly, they remain silent.   Later, mathematics assumed the role of instrument of selection.   And we know that many children are still punished for counting with their fingers!

How to explain what occurs with peoples, communities, and individuals when they encounter the strange, the different, the unfamiliar.   Every individual carries with him/her cultural roots that come from their home, from the day they were born.   They learn from their parents, friends, neighbors, community.   The individual spends many years acquiring these roots.   Upon arriving in school, there is normally a process of refinement, transformation, and substitution of these roots, very similar to that which occurs in the process of religious conversion.

The moment of cultural encounter has a very complex dynamic. This encounter occurs between peoples, as occurred in the conquest and colonization, between groups.   It also occurs in the encounter between the young man or woman, who have their own cultural roots, and the other culture, the culture of the school, with which the teacher identifies. The civilizing process, and we could say the same of the school process, is essentially the management of this dynamic.

The school dynamic could also have creative and positive results, which manifest themselves in the creation of the new. But generally, negative and perverse results are noted, which manifest themselves, above all, in the exercise of power and the elimination or exclusion of the dominated.

Conversion depends on the individual forgetting or even rejecting her roots. But an individual without roots is like a tree without roots or a house without a foundation: it is blown over with the first wind. Individuals without solid roots become more fragile, and do not resist harassment. The individual needs a reference, which is situated not on the roots of others, but on their own roots. Without roots, he grasps onto the other when he falls, and embarks on a process of dependence, which is fertile ground for the perverse manifestation of power of one individual over another.

We are witnessing this process in school systems and in society. It is the power of those who know more, who have more, who *can* more. What feeds the power of the dominator? This power can only have continuity if someone depends on him, the dominator grasps onto to him. And who is going to grasp onto him? Without a doubt, those who have no roots.

This was the efficient strategy adopted by the colonizer: eliminate the historicity of the conquered, i.e., eliminate their roots. The process of de-colonization, which celebrates with the adoption of a flag, a hymn, a constitution, is incomplete if the cultural roots of the colonized are not recognized.

Ethnomathematics fits into this reflection about de-colonization and the search for real possibilities of access for the subordinated, the marginalized, and the outcast, or excluded. The most promising strategy for education in societies that are in transition from subordination to autonomy is to restore dignity to their individuals, recognizing and respecting their roots. Recognizing and respecting an individual's roots does not signify rejecting the roots of the other, but rather in a process of synthesis, reinforcing their own roots. This is, according to my thinking, the most important aspect of ethnomathematics.

THE EDUCATIONAL DIMENSION

The ethnomathematical proposal does not signify the rejection of academic mathematics, as suggested by the unfortunate title of an excellent article about ethnomathematics published in the *Chronicle of Higher Education*, "*Good Bye, Pythagoras*", that I mentioned in the Introduction. It is not about ignoring nor rejecting the academic mathematics symbolized by Pythagoras. Due to historical circumstances, like it or not, the peoples who, beginning in the 16th Century, conquered and colonized the entire planet were successful thanks to the knowledge and behavior that was founded in Pythagoras and his companions from the Mediterranean Basin. This is the knowledge and behavior that, incorporated into modernity, guides our daily lives today. This is not about ignoring nor rejecting modern knowledge and behavior, but rather perfecting them, incorporating values of humanity, synthesized into an ethics of respect, solidarity, and cooperation.

Knowing and assimilating the culture of the dominator can become positive as long as the roots of the dominated are strong. In mathematics education, ethnomathematics can strengthen these roots.

From a utilitarian point of view, which cannot be ignored as a very important goal of school, it is a big mistake to think that ethnomathematics can substitute **good academic mathematics**, which is essential for an individual to be an active being in the modern world. In modern society, ethnomathematics will have limited utility, but at the same time, much of academic mathematics is absolutely useless in this society, as well.

When I say **good academic mathematics**, I am excluding that which is uninteresting, obsolete, and useless, which, unfortunately, dominates current programs. It is obvious that we will obtain **good academic mathematics** if we do away with much of what continues to be included in programs with no other justification beyond a damaging conservatism and an unsustainable propeadeutical character. We often hear, "It is necessary to learn **this** to have a basis to be able to learn **that**." The fact is, the "that" should be dropped, and more still, the "this".

For example, it is inadmissible today to think about arithmetic and algebra, which privilege quantitative reasoning, without the full use of calculators. Quantitative reasoning made possible the great advances in mathematics, beginning in the late Middle Ages, thanks to resorting to quantification of the results of experiments which eventually came to dominate mathematics education.[13] Quantitative reasoning was the reason for the existence of calculators and computers. And now, the greatest educational accomplishment of quantitative reasoning, calculus [arithmetic, algebraic, differential, integral] is integrated with calculators and computers.[14]

On the other hand, qualitative reasoning, also known as analytical, which is strongly conceptual and had regained momentum at the beginning of the 17th Century, gained importance in the modern world, giving rise to new fields of mathematics that developed in the second half of the 20th Century, such as statistics, probabilities, programming, modeling, *fuzzies*, and fractals. Currently, one of the most active fields of research, artificial intelligence, aims to incorporate qualitative reasoning into computers.

It may seem contradictory to speak about such sophisticated mathematics as *fuzzies* and fractals when we make the ethnomathematics proposal. But this is precisely the essence of ethnomathematics: incorporating the mathematics of the cultural moment, contextualized, into mathematics education. Fractals are, today, part of the popular imagination and curiosity. They awaken the interest of children, youth, and adults.[15]

Qualitative reasoning is essential to arrive at a new organization of society, as it permits the exercise of criticism and analysis of the world in which we live. It should, without further hesitation, be incorporated into educational systems. This incorporation occurs through the introduction into these programs, at all academic levels, of statistics, probability, programming, modeling, *fuzzies*, fractals, and other new, emerging fields of current science.

Ethnomathematics privileges qualitative reasoning. An ethnomathematical focus is always linked to a larger question, of an environmental nature or of production, and ethnomathematics rarely appears disassociated from other cultural manifestations, such as art and religion. Ethnomathematics fits perfectly into a multicultural and holistic conception of education.

Multiculturalism is becoming the most notable characteristic of education today. With the great mobility of people and families, intercultural relations will become more intense. Intercultural encounters will generate conflicts that can only be resolved based on ethics that result from the individual knowing him/herself and knowing his/her culture, and respecting the culture of the other.

Respect will come from knowing. In any other manner, behavior will reveal arrogance, superiority, and prepotency, which inevitably result in confrontation and violence.

The absolute priority of our mission as educators is to obtain PEACE in future generations. We cannot forget that these generations will live in a multicultural environment, that their relations will be intercultural, and their day-to-day lives will be impregnated with technology. Perhaps humans will co-exist with cloned and transgenic individuals, or even androids. A scenario of fiction, as we see in films such as *Blade Runner* and *Matrix*, can become reality. We do not yet know how to deal with this. It is future generations that will organize the world of the future. Today we do not yet know what to do in a future that reveals itself with facts that are still in the realm of fiction, but that are rapidly becoming reality.

How can we teach them to build their world of peace and happiness? The future will be built by them. What can we offer them so that they can build a future without the evils of the present? The manner in which past generations dealt with the future, anchored in all the knowledge modernity offered, gave us our present; a distressful present, of inequality, injustice, arrogance, exclusion, environmental destruction, inter- and intra-cultural conflicts, wars. This is not the legacy we should leave to our great grandchildren and future generations.

As educators, we can offer the children of today, who constitute the generation that will, in twenty or thirty years, be in decision making positions, a critical vision of the present, and the intellectual and material instruments that we have at our disposal for this critique. We are experiencing a profound transition, with more intensity than in any other period in history, of communication, of economic models and production systems, and of systems of governance and decision making.

Education in this transition cannot focus on the mere transmission of obsolete content, for the most part uninteresting and useless, and inconsequential for the construction of a new society. What we can do for our children is offer them the communicative, analytic, and material instruments for them to live with a capacity for criticism in a multicultural society impregnated with technology. [16]

Mathematics imposed itself as a strong presence in all fields of knowledge, and in all actions of the modern world. Its presence in the future will certainly be intensified, but not in the form practiced today. It will no doubt be an integral part of communicative, analytic, and material instruments.The dynamic acquisition of mathematics integrated with the knowledge and practices of the future depends on offering students enriching experiences. It is up to the teacher of the future to idealize, organize, and facilitate these experiences. But for this, the teacher must be prepared with another dynamic. As Beatriz D'Ambrosio said, "the future mathematics teacher should learn new mathematical ideas in an alternative way".[17]

I see our great mission as educators to be the preparation of a happy future. And, as mathematics educators, we must be in step with the great mission of the educator. The mathematics educator who fails to perceive that there is much more to his mission as educator than teaching how to add and subtract or solve equations and problems that are absolutely artificial, even though they often appear to refer to real facts, is, in the least, mistaken.

The pedagogical proposal of ethnomathematics is to bring mathematics to life, dealing with real situations in time [now] and space [here]; and, through criticism, to question the here and now. Upon doing so, we plunge into cultural roots and practice cultural dynamics. We are effectively recognizing the importance, in education, of the various cultures and traditions in the formation of a new civilization that is transcultural and transdisciplinary.

As Teresa Vergani said,

> Ethnomathematics knows that an *unitary and plural world* is being generated, and that the undoing of the blockade between cultures begins with tending to the problem of reciprocal 'translatability'.
>
> The first hybrid characteristic of ethnomathematics to take into account is its *engagement in the dialogue between identity (world) and alterity (local), terrain where mathematics and anthropology intersect.*[18]

For all these reasons, I see ethnomathematics as a path to a renovated education, able to prepare future generations to build a happier civilization. To attain this civilization, that I dream of and that I believe can be reached, it is necessary to attain PEACE, in its various dimensions: individual, social, environmental, and military.

The United Nations, through UNESCO, has proclaimed the decade that dawns before us as the Decade for a Culture of Peace and Non-Violence. All educational efforts should be directed toward this priority. Ethnomathematics is a response to this appeal.

CHAPTER 3

THE COGNITIVE DIMENSION:
KNOWLEDGE AND BEHAVIOR

KNOWLEDGE AND ACTION

The intellectual and social generation of knowledge, and its diffusion, provide the general framework in which I seek to develop my specific proposals for mathematics education. The ideas presented here may appear to be somewhat vague, imprecise, and exploratory. This reflects what could be called "the state of the art" of the theory of knowledge. We know very little about how we think. Traditional programs that include courses in psychology, learning, and related topics have become obsolete in light of recent contributions from cybernetics, artificial intelligence, and neurology.[1]

Throughout history, one can recognize the efforts of individuals and of all societies to find explanations and ways of coping and living with the natural and socio-cultural reality. This gave origin to modes of communication and languages, religions, and arts, as well as the sciences and mathematics – ultimately, to everything we call knowledge. Individuals, and the species as a whole, stand out among their peers and reach their potential for creativity because they know. All knowledge is the result of a long, cumulative process in which stages can be identified, naturally not dichotomous among themselves, when the generation, intellectual organization, social organization, and diffusion of knowledge take place.

These stages are, respectively, the object of the theory of cognition, of epistemology, of history and sociology, and of education and politics. As a whole, this process is extremely dynamic and never-ending, and is obviously subject to very specific conditions of stimulus and subordination to the natural, cultural, and social context. Thus is the cycle of individual and social acquisition of knowledge.

My reflections on multicultural education have led me to see the generation of knowledge as primordial in this whole process. The truth is, this generation occurs in the present, in the moment of transition between the past and the future. That is, the acquisition

37

and elaboration of knowledge occur in the present, as a result of an entire past, individual and cultural, projected into the future. The future is understood as immediate and, at the same time, very remote. As a result, reality is modified, incorporating new facts into it, i.e., "artifacts" and "mentifacts". This behavior is intrinsic to the human being, and results from the drives for survival and transcendence.

Although a process of knowledge construction can be recognized here, my proposal is broader than constructivism, which becomes effectively a pedagogical proposal, with structuralist characteristics, privileging the rational. The holistic focus that I propose incorporates the sensorial, the intuitive, the emotional, and the rational through the individual will for survival and transcendence. This proposal is in tune, to a degree, with the philosophy of education of Comenius.[2]

As I mentioned previously, I see survival and transcendence as the essence of being [verb] human. The human being [noun], like all living species, seeks only to survive. The will to transcend is the most distinctive feature of our species.

It is not known from where the will to survive as an individual and as a species comes. Without a doubt, it is incorporated into the genetic mechanism from the beginning of life. It is simply known that this force is the essence of all living species. No species, and therefore, no individual, is oriented by their own extinction. Each moment is an exercise in survival.

Equally, we do not know how the human species acquired the will to transcend, which also appears to be embedded on our genetic code. This has been the greatest philosophical question in the entire history of humanity and in all cultures. In the form of soul, will, free will, the drive to transcend the moment of survival is recognized in various manifestations of the human being.

Reflections on the present, like the realization of our will to survive and to transcend, should necessarily be of a transdisciplinary and holist nature. In this view, the present, which presents itself as the interface between the past and the future, is associated with action and practice.[3]

The focus of our study is man, as in integrated individual, immersed in a natural and social environment, which signifies permanent interaction with his natural and socio-cultural environment. The present is when the [inter]action of the individual with her natural and socio-cultural environment manifests itself, which I call behavior. Behavior, which we also call practice, doing, or action, is identified with the present. The behavior determines the theory, which is the set of organized explanations that result from a reflection on doing. The theories and the elaboration of systems of explanation is what we generally call knowing, or simply, knowledge. In fact, knowledge is the substrate of behavior, which is the essence of being alive.

The vital cycle . . . → REALITY → INDIVIDUAL → ACTION → . . . can be diagrammed as follows:

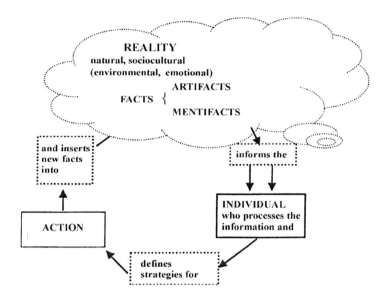

Figure 2.

This cycle is permanent, which permits every human being to interact with his environment, with the reality considered in its totality as a complex of natural and artificial facts. This action occurs through the processing of information gathered from reality by a processor that constitutes a true cybernetic complex, with a multiplicity of non-dichotomous sensors, identified through instinct, memory, reflections, emotions, fantasy, intuition, and other elements that we can scarcely imagine. As Oliver Sacks observes, referring especially to visual perception, but which applies to all the senses:

We achieve perceptive constancy – the correlation of all the different appearances, the modifications of objects – very early, in the first months of life. We are speaking of an enormous learning task, but which is accomplished so smoothly, so unconsciously, that its immense complexity is barely noticed (despite being a feat that not even the greatest supercomputers can begin to take on).[4]

The interaction of the individual with reality, of which she is an integral part and agent of transformations, is a great challenge to the sciences of cognition, particularly of artificial intelligence. As Humberto Maturana said,

> human beings do not exist in a domain of independent entities and relations; rather we exist in a domain of entities and relations that result in operational coherences of our operation as human beings.

Further on, Maturana distinguishes mathematics from other forms of knowing:

> Mathematical formalisms do not apply to an independent reality; they apply to coherences of our living to the extent that they embody configurations of relations that are isomorphic with the operations that we execute when we live.[5]

GOING BEYOND SURVIVAL

The processing of information (input) results in strategies for action (output). In other words, man executes his vital cycle of behavior/knowledge not only because of the animal motivation to survive; he subordinates this cycle to transcendence, through the consciousness of doing/knowing, i.e., he does because he knows, and knows because he is doing. And this has its effect on reality, creating new interpretations and uses of the natural and artificial reality, modifying it through the introduction of new facts, artifacts and mentifacts. Although it closely approximates the nomenclature abstract/concrete, I prefer artifact/mentifact, as abstract and concrete refer to the manner of collecting facts, whereas when we speak of artifact and mentifact, we are referring to the generation of facts. Knowledge is what generates knowing, which is decisive for action, and subsequently, it is in the behavior, the practice, the doing that one evaluates, redefines, and reconstructs knowledge. Consciousness is what impels the action of man toward survival and transcendence, as he knows through doing, and does because he knows. The process of acquiring knowledge is, thus, this dialectic relation between knowing/doing, impelled by consciousness, and is achieved in various dimensions.

Of the various dimensions of the acquisition of knowledge, we highlight four, which are the most widely recognized and interpreted in theories of knowledge: sensorial, intuitive, emotional, and rational. Generally, religious knowledge is associated with the intuitive and emotional dimensions, whereas scientific knowledge is favored by the rational, and the emotional prevails in the arts. Naturally, these dimensions are not dichotomous nor hierarchical, but rather complementary. Just as there is no dichotomy between knowing and doing, there is also no prioritization of one over another, nor does one dimension of the process prevail over another. Each one complements the other in a whole that is behavior and that results in knowledge.

Consequently, the dichotomies body/mind, material/spirit, manual/intellectual, and so many others that have impregnated themselves in modern thought, are artifacts.

In the last 50 years, impressive development can be noted in the modern science of cognition, which is an amalgam of, among other things, psychology, biology, artificial intelligence, linguistics, philosophy. One observes, when compared to experimental psychology, excessive attention given to internal mental processes. Today, cognitive science itself seeks to understand the factors that permit interaction of the subjects with their environment. One example is the so-called personified cognitive science. Thus emerges the emotional robot!

Two robots are being created in the Laboratory of Artificial Intelligence at the Massachusetts Institute of Technology: Cog, which is an analog of a child, and learns to coordinate its movements to explore its environment; and Kismet, built to interact with humans through body posture and facial expressions. It is interesting to note that there is a theologian participating in the project whose presence is justified by a number of questions: What does it mean to be human? Are our reactions developed in a mechanical, functionalist manner? Or is there a social dimension associated with our reactions? The ethical questions are innumerable.[6] These are basic questions for studies about knowledge and human behavior, one of the principle objectives of ethnomathematics.

The new perception regarding the nature of cognition offered to us by the new research field known as Artificial Intelligence is intriguing and challenging for education.

Ignorance of the new views of cognition has a perverse reflection in pedagogical practices which refuse, possibly because of this ignorance, to accept technology. There is still enormous resistance on the part of educators, mathematics educators in particular, to technology. The most damaging case is resistance to the use of the calculator.[7] Computers and the Internet are both equally ignored in mathematics curricula. Clearly, the introduction of calculators and computers is not merely a question of methodology. As a function of available technology, new objects for mathematics education emerge, and new subjects, as well, that could never be addressed without information technologies. Often resistance comes imbibed with an obsolete ideological discourse that makes it difficult to overcome the evils of perverse capitalism which can be identified in the form of the inequality, arrogance, and prepotency so common in today's schools.

Many will be thinking at this point that I am straying from ethnomathematics. On the contrary. I remember fractals, which from the pedagogical as well as the cultural point of view, are very attractive to children. It is interest to consider Ron Eglash's study of architecture, urbanization, weaving, and even body decorations, such as tattoos and hair styles, of African cultures. One notes in all of these cases the presence of a fractal structure, well-studied by Eglash.[8]

FROM THE INDIVIDUAL TO THE COLLECTIVE

The present, as an interface between the past and the future, manifests itself in action. The present is thus identified as behavior, has the same dynamic as behavior, i.e., is informed by the past, is a result of the history of the individual and the collectivity, of previous knowledge, individual and collective, conditioned by the projection on the future; all beginning with the information provided by reality. In reality are stored all the facts that inform the individual[s].

The information is processed by the individual[s] and results in strategies for action. As a result of these actions, new facts (artifacts and/or mentifacts) are incorporated into reality, obviously modifying it, becoming stored in the collection of facts that constitute it. Reality is, therefore, undergoing incessant modification. The past is thus projected, through the intermediation of individuals, into the future. Once again, the past/future dichotomy is seen as artificial, as the instant that comes from the past and projects itself into the future thus acquires a transdimensionality that we could think of as a fold (a *pli* in the sense of the catastrophes of René Thom[9]). This re-thinking of the dimensionality of the instant gives to life, including the "instants" of birth and death, a character of continuity, of fusion, in an instant, of the past and of the future.

We recognize, however, that there can be no frozen present, as there is no static action, as there is no behavior without instant feedback (evaluation) based on its effects. Thus, behavior is the link between reality, which informs, and action, which modifies it.

Action generates knowledge, that is, the capacity to explain, cope with, manage, understand reality. This capacity is transmitted and accumulated horizontally, in the company of others, contemporaries, through communications, and vertically, from each individual to him/herself (memory), and from each generation to the next (historical memory). Note that it is through what we call memory, which is a form of information of the same nature as sensorial mechanisms, that genetic information and the unconscious, that the experiences of an individual in the past, are incorporated into reality and inform this individual in the same way as other facts of reality.

The individual is not alone. There are billions of other individuals of the same species with the same vital cycle ". . . REALITY informs the INDIVIDUAL who processes and carries out an ACTION that modifies REALITY that informs the INDIVIDUAL . . .", and also billions of individuals of other species with their own behavior, carrying out a similar vital cycle, all incessantly contributing a piece to modify reality. The individual is inserted in a cosmic reality, like a link between all of history, from the beginning of time and of things until the moment, the here and now.[10] All the experiences of the past, recognized and identified or not, constitute reality in its totality, and determine an aspect of behavior of each individual. Their action results from processing retrieved information. This includes the experiences of each individual and the experiences in their totality, including those of all individuals who ever lived, most of which are not retrievable. The recovery of these experiences (individual memory, cultural memory, genetic memory) constitutes one of the challenges of psychoanalysis, of history, and of innumerable other sciences. It even constitutes the basis for certain modes of explanation (arts and religions). In a temporal duality, these same aspects of behavior manifest themselves in strategies of action that will result in new facts – artifacts and mentifacts – that will take place in the future, and which, once generated, will incorporate themselves into reality.

Strategies for action are motivated by the projection of the individual into the future (her desires, ambitions, motivations, and so many other factors), in the near future, as well as the distant future. This is the meaning of transcendence to which I referred above.

Each individual's process of generating knowledge as action based on information gathered from reality is also experienced by the other, in the same instant. Reality is perceived differently, i.e. the information received by each individual is different. Consequently, the behavior and knowledge are different, and often conflicting. The moments experienced by the two individuals present are mutually enriching, thanks to communication, which allows both to have information enriched by the information communicated to him by the other.

The discovery of the other, and of others, present or from the past, is essential for the phenomenon of life. Although the mechanisms of gathering information and processing this information, defining strategies for action, are absolutely individual, and remain as such, they are enriched by mutual exposition and communication, which is effectively a pact (contract) between individuals. The establishment of this pact is an essential phenomenon for the continuity of life.

Particularly in the human species, it is communication that permits the definition of strategies for common action. This does not assume the elimination of each individual's own capacity for action, inherent to her will (free will), but may inhibit certain actions; in other words, the common action that results from information can be interpreted as *in*action, resulting from the pact. Thus, through communication, actions desirable to both may originate and inhibit actions, i.e. in-actions are generated that are undesirable for one or both parties. In this way, it becomes possible to live together in society.

I insist on the fact that these mechanisms of inhibition do not transform each individual's own mechanisms of gathering and processing information. Each individual has these mechanisms, and it is this that maintains the individuality and identity of each being.

No one is the same as the other in their capacity to gather and process information at the same instant, immersed in the same reality.

These notions can easily be generalized to the group, the community, and a people, through social communication and a social pact which, I insist, takes into account the capacity of each individual, and does not eliminate the will of each individual, i.e., their free will. The knowledge generated by common interaction, resulting from social communication, will be a complex of codes and symbols that are intellectually and socially organized, constituting knowledge shared by the group.

In the same way, the behavior generated by common interaction resulting from social communication will be subordinated to parameters that translate the pact to manifest actions that are desirable for all and inhibit actions that are undesirable for one or both parties. The set of these parameters constitutes a value system of the group that permits "compatibilized" behavior.

The symbiotic association of shared knowledge and compatibilized behaviors constitutes what we call culture.

The culture is manifested in the complex of *saberes/fazeres* [knowledge/practices], in communication, in the values agreed upon by a group, community, or people. Culture is what is going to allow life in society.

When societies and, therefore, cultural systems, encounter each other and mutually expose themselves, they are subject to a dynamic of interaction that produces intercultural behavior that one notes in groups of individuals, in communities, in tribes, and in societies as a whole. The results of this dynamic of the encounter are the intercultural manifestations that have been intensifying throughout the history of humanity.

In some cases, the domination of one system over another takes place in the encounter; sometimes, the substitution of one system by another; and even the suppression or total elimination of a system; but in the majority of cases, the result is the generation of new systems of explanation. Even though dominated by emotional tensions, the relations between individuals of the same culture (intracultural), and above all, the relations between individuals of different cultures (intercultural), represent the creative potential of the species. Just as biodiversity represents the path to the emergence of new species, the potential creativity of humanity resides in cultural diversity.

ETHNOMATHEMATICS

The above presentation synthesizes the theoretical foundations that serve as the basis for a research program about the generation, intellectual organization, social organization, and diffusion of knowledge. In the language of disciplines, it could be said to be an interdisciplinary program involving what constitutes the domain of the so-called sciences of cognition, epistemology, history, sociology, and of diffusion, which includes education.

Methodologically, this program recognizes that the behavior of the species *homo sapiens sapiens*, in its adventure as a planetary species, like the other species that preceded it, i.e. the various hominids recognized from 4.5 million years before the present, was informed by the acquisition of knowledge and practices that allowed them to survive and transcend through ways, modes, techniques and arts of explaining, knowing, understanding, and coping with, of living together with, the natural and sociocultural reality in which they are inserted.

Naturally, in all cultures and in all times, knowledge, which is generated by the need for a response to distinct problems and situations, is subordinated to a natural, social, and cultural context.

Throughout history and throughout their existence, individuals and peoples have created and developed instruments for reflection and observation, material and intellectual instruments [which I call **tics**] to explain, understand, come to know, and learn to know and do [which I call **mathema**] in response to the needs for survival and transcendence in different natural, social, and cultural environments [which I call **ethno**]. Thus, from this derives the name Ethnomathematics.

The name suggests an academically recognized body of knowledge, like mathematics. In fact, in all cultures, we find manifestations related, and even identified, with what we call mathematics today (that is, processes of organizing, classifying, counting, measuring, and inferring), generally mixed together with, or difficult to distinguish from, other forms that today are identified as art, religion, music, techniques, sciences. In all times, and in all cultures, mathematics, arts, religion, music, techniques, sciences were developed with the aim of explaining, knowing, learning, of knowing/doing, and of predicting the future (divination arts). They all appear mixed together and indistinguishable as forms of knowledge in an initial stage of the history of humanity and in the personal life of each of us.

We are living in a period in which the means of gathering information, and each individual's processing of information, find in communications and in computer technology, auxiliary instruments of a scope unimaginable in other times. Interaction between individuals also finds, in telephone technology, a great potential, as yet difficult to appreciate, to generate common actions.

In education, we are seeing growing recognition of the importance of intercultural relations. However, there is still, unfortunately, a reluctance to recognize intracultural relations. There is still an insistence upon placing children in grades according to their age, offering the same curriculum in the same grade, even going so far as to propose national curricula. Even more absurd is the evaluation of groups of individuals using standardized tests. This effectively amounts to an attempt to pasteurize new generations! The plurality of means of mass communication, facilitated by transportation, has taken intercultural relations to truly interplanetary dimensions.

Thus begins a new era that opens up enormous possibilities for planetary behavior and knowledge, with unprecedented results for understanding and harmony for all of humanity – not for the biological nor cultural homogenization of the species, but rather for the harmonious co-existence of the different, through an ethic of mutual respect, solidarity, and cooperation.

Different ways of explanation, understanding, coping with, and living with reality have always existed. But now, thanks to new means of communication and transportation, the differences are noted with greater evidence, creating the need for a behavior that transcends even the new cultural forms. Eventually, the free will that is so desired, peculiar to being [verb] human, will be able to manifest itself in a model of "transculturality" that will allow each individual to achieve fulfillment.

An appropriate model to facilitate this new stage of evolution of our species is so-called multi-cultural education, which has been imposing itself in education systems around the world.

We know that, at the moment, there are more than 200 states and approximately 6,000 indigenous nations in the world, with a population totaling between 10–15% of the total population of the world. Although it is not my objective to discuss indigenous education, the contributions of specialists in the field have been very

47

important for understanding how education can be an instrument to reinforce mechanisms of social exclusion.

It is important to remember that practically all countries, including Brazil, subscribe to the Declaration of New Delhi (December 16, 1993), which is explicit in recognizing that

> education is the preeminent instrument for promoting universal human values, quality of human resources, and respect for cultural diversity (2.2)

and that

> the contents and methods of education need to be developed to serve the basic learning needs of individuals and societies, providing them with the power to face their most urgent problems – combat poverty, increase productivity, improve conditions for life, and protect the environment – and allowing them to assume their rightful role in the construction of democratic societies and the enrichment of their cultural heritage (2.4).

Nothing could be clearer in this declaration than the recognition of the subordination of programmatic contents to cultural diversity. Equally, the recognition of a variety of learning styles is implicit in the appeal for the development of new methods.

Essentially, these considerations determine an enormous flexibility, in the selection of contents as well as the methodology of teaching.

This approach to distinct ways of knowing is the essence of the Program Ethnomathematics. The truth is, unlike what the name suggests, ethnomathematics is not simply the study of the "mathematics of diverse ethnic groups". To repeat what I have already written in many other works, as well as other parts of this book, in order to compose the word ethnomathematics, I used the roots *tics, mathema,* and *ethno* to signify that there are various ways, techniques, abilities (*tics*) to explain, understand, deal with, and live with (*mathema*) distinct natural and socio-cultural contexts of reality (*ethno*). What are the implications of this program for the organization of a curriculum?

48

SCHOOL AND CURRICULUM

great!

I use a very broad definition of curriculum. Curriculum is a strategy for educational action. Throughout history, the curriculum is organized as a reflection of national priorities and the interests of the groups that are in power. Much more than the academic importance of disciplines, the curriculum reflects what society expects of the respective disciplines that compose it. I will focus on the way mathematics appears in educational systems and in the curriculum.

We inherited from the Romans an institutional model that still prevails in modern society, in education, in particular. In the Roman world, the curriculum that corresponds today to primary education was organized as a *trivium*, including the disciplines of grammar, rhetoric, and dialectics. The great motivator for this curriculum was the consolidation of the Roman Empire, dependent on a strong concept of citizenship.

In the Middle Ages, with the expansion of Christianity, other educational needs were created. This is reflected in the organization of what would become secondary education, of more advanced studies. The curricular organization was denominated *quadrivium*, and included the disciplines of arithmetic, music, geometry, and astronomy. As with the *trivium*, this curricular organization found its reason for being in the socio-cultural and economic moment of the time.

Modern science, originating in the Mediterranean cultures, began to delineate itself at the same time as the great navigational explorations, the conquest and colonization, and soon imposed itself as a prototype of rational knowledge, and substrate of the efficient and fascinating modern technology. Originating from the central nations, structured and dichotomous conceptualizations of knowing [knowledge] and doing [abilities] became defined.

The great advances in styles of explanation of natural facts and economy, which characterized European thought beginning in the 16th Century, created a demand for new goals for education.[11] The principle goal was to create a school that was accessible to all and responded to a new social and economic order. As Comenius said:

> If, therefore, we want orderly, thriving churches and states and good administrations, first of all, we order the schools and make them thrive, in order for them to be true and live

workshops of men, and ecclesiastical, political and economic nurseries. [12]

This could be said to be the origin of Modern Didactics, reflecting the needs of the emergent colonialism.

The new ideas in education anticipated the needs of the three great revolutions of the 17th Century: the Industrial Revolution, which profoundly altered the system of production and of property; the American Revolution, which created a new model for choosing leaders of a nation; and the French Revolution, which recognized inalienable rights of every human being.

The great political and economic transformations that resulted in the three revolutions caused profound changes in educational systems. As in other times, the interests of the empires were determinants. Particularly remarkable are the educational changes that occurred in France under Napoleon, and in Germany under Bismarck, particularly in higher education.

Without a doubt, the model that best responded to the needs of the colonies which, in the path opened up by the American Revolution, conquered their independence, was that adopted by the United States of America. In the first years of its existence as an independent nation, the objective was the occupation of the territory, i.e. the fixation of a population of European immigrants on the native lands conquered in the *Indian Wars* during the great expansion westward. The European immigrants had to face new situations and, at the same time, become integrated in a vast territory. Coming from the most varied origins, assuming a new national identity and creating a new tradition was the priority. The American model aimed for a school that was equal for all and offered a basic curriculum, which became known as "the three R's: Reading, wRiting, and aRithmetic". Higher public education, the land-grant colleges, aimed to give the immigrants the means to develop autonomous systems of production.

Reading, writing, and arithmetic prevailed in the old colonial metropolises and in the new independent countries. It was suitable for the period of transition from manual production to an incipient technology, and for the formation of new nationalities in the 19th Century. With the emergence of more advanced technology, which is the great characteristic of the transition from the 19th to the 20th Centuries, another type of employee, functionary, or worker became necessary. Reading, writing, and arithmetic were obviously insufficient for the incoming century.

Thus, the great reforms and new educational proposals began. Particularly affected was the teaching of the sciences and of mathematics. The foundations of a New School arise, and Mathematics Education emerges as a new discipline.

THE TRANSITION FROM THE 20TH TO THE 21ST CENTURIES

In modern society, dominated by technology, profoundly affected by globalization, and in which the greatest priority is the pursuit of peace in its multiple dimensions, literacy and counting, albeit necessary, are insufficient for the full exercise of citizenship.

A good education should not be evaluated by the content taught by the teacher and learned by the student. The worn out educational paradigm synthesized in the "teaching-learning" binomial, verified by inept evaluations, is unsustainable.[13] One would expect education to make possible, for the one being educated, the acquisition and utilization of the communicative, analytic, and material instruments that will be essential for the exercise of all the rights and responsibilities intrinsic to citizenship.

Focusing on the organization of knowledge and behaviors that will be necessary for full citizenship, I recently proposed a *trivium* for the era that we are entering, based on the concepts of **literacy, matheracy, and technoracy.**[14] I believe that this new conceptualization of curriculum will respond to the demands of the modern world.

My proposal is an educational response to the expectations of eliminating inequity and violations of human dignity, the first step for social justice. The words literacy, matheracy, and technoracy can be considered neologisms, although they have occasionally appeared in the educational literature.

I propose some definitions that broaden the way these neologisms are used when they occasionally appear in English, regarding the use of literacy and matheracy.[15] I have seen *technological literacy*, but never *technoracy*.

My conception is:

LITERACY: the capacity to process written and spoken information, which includes reading, writing, calculations, dialogue, media, and the Internet in everyday lives [**Communicative Instruments**].

MATHERACY: the capacity to interpret and analyze signs and codes, propose and utilize models and simulations in everyday life, elaborate abstractions based on representations of the real [**Analytical Instruments**].

TECHNORACY: the capacity to use and combine instruments, simple or complex, including one's own body, evaluating their possibilities and limitations and their adaptation to diverse needs and situations [**Material Instruments**].

We are not talking here about introducing new disciplines or putting new labels on that which already exists. The proposal is to organize teaching strategies, which we call curriculum, along the lines of what I call literacy, materacy, and technoracy. This is the response to what we know today about the human mind and behavior. As I sought to show in this chapter, the Program Ethnomathematics reflects what we know today about the human mind and society.

CHAPTER 4

ETHNOMATHEMATICS IN A CHANGING CIVILIZATION

THE HOLISTIC NATURE OF EDUCATION

Education, in general, depends on variables that group themselves in broad directions:
   a) the student who is in the educational process as an individual seeking to achieve her aspirations and respond to her inquietudes;
   b) her insertion in society and society's expectations regarding her;
   c) the strategies of this society to accomplish these expectations;
   d) the agents and instruments to carry out these strategies;
   e) the content that is part of this strategy.

In general, the analysis of these variables has been the domain of a few academic specialties: a) → learning and cognition; b) → objectives and philosophy of education; c) → teaching and structure and functioning of the school; d) → teacher education and methodology; e) → contents.
   Unfortunately, in our teacher education programs, as well as graduate programs, there has been a reductionist emphasis on some of these specialties, to the exclusion of the others. Thus is created the figure of specialists, with their specific areas of expertise. It is incumbent upon the psychologists to concern themselves with "a", the philosophers with "b", the pedagogues "c" and "d", and the mathematicians, "e". As if it were possible to separate these fields!
   The preceding chapters pointed toward a holistic approach to mathematics education. To speak of a holistic approach always evokes shudders from the reader or listener; like talking about transdisciplinarity, a systemic focus, globalization, multiculturalism, and ETHNOMATHEMATICS.
   The approach to distinct ways of knowing is the essence of the Program Ethnomathematics. As should have become clear in the preceding chapters, ethnomathematics is not simply the study of the "mathematics of diverse ethnic groups". As has already been

53

explained, to compose the word **ethno mathema tics**, I used the roots *tics, mathema,* and *ethno* to signify that there are various ways, techniques, abilities (**tics**) of explaining, understanding, coping with, and living with (**mathema**) distinct natural and socioeconomic contexts of reality (**ethno**).

TOWARD A PLANETARY CIVILIZATION

We are headed towards a planetary civilization in which sharing knowledge and making behavior compatible cannot remain restricted to specific cultures [intraculturalism] nor to exchanges of the cultural dynamic itself [interculturalism]. Knowledge and behavior in the planetary civilization will be transcultural: transdisciplinary knowledge and behavior subordinated to a larger ethic.

And what might this larger ethic be? Humanity, in this current phase of transition to a planetary civilization, is going through an ethical crisis. It is not only about a crisis of values, which is, without a doubt, of great concern and affects our daily lives. Life is the result of three facts: the individual, the other, and nature. The continuity of life as a cosmic phenomenon depends on the resolution of the triangle

Individual ⟷ Nature

Others / Society

The facts, that is, the individual, the other(s), and nature, and the relations between them, are indissoluble; one does not exist without the other. Like a triangle, the vertices and sides are integrated and indissoluble. One vertex cannot be resolved without the other; one vertex, or one side, is not the triangle.

The big problems confronting humanity are situated in the relations [sides] between the individual, the other(s), and nature [vertices]. Equilibrium and harmonization of these relations constitutes a larger ethic that I call the **ethic of diversity**. Peace, in its multiple dimensions [military, environmental, social, interior] is the realization, in everyday life, of this ethic. [1]

The great crisis that humanity is going through is situated in the lack of equilibrium of these relations, which manifests itself in arrogance, prepotency, inequality, indifference, violence, and innumerable problems that affect our daily lives.

Mathematics, as a form of knowledge, has everything to do with ethics and, consequently, with peace.[2] The search for new directions for the development of mathematics should be incorporated with mathematical "doing". Duly revitalized, mathematics, as it is practiced today in the academic environment and research organizations, will continue to be the most important intellectual instrument to explain, understand, innovate, and aid, principally to solve the greatest problems that are affecting humanity. It will no doubt be necessary to re-open the question of foundations, evidently a vulnerable point of current mathematics.[3]

Mathematics education is deeply affected by priorities of this period of transition to a planetary civilization. The pursuit of equity in the society of the future, where cultural diversity will be the norm, demands an attitude without arrogance and prepotency in education, particularly in mathematics education.[4] When I speak of equity, I am not referring to the Principle of Equity, defended by a panel of mathematics educators and mathematicians: "Mathematics can and should be learned by all students."[5] This principle responds to the ideal of the continuity of our current society, competitive and exclusive, using instruments of selection that are subordinated to mathematics. This conceptualization of equity carries with it, necessarily, the figure of the excluded, the oucast. The ideal that I defend is the non-existence of excluded people. Perhaps what would be most appropriate is a *fuzzy* mathematics education, a term that has been widely used in the so-called *math wars* among factions of mathematics educators and mathematicians.

Analyzing the state of current civilization, globalization is undeniable and inevitable. Above all, the means of transportation and communication, and systems of production, become irreversible, and the process of globalization foretells the planetary society. Notwithstanding, we are experiencing a civilization dominated by the market of capital, in a form of perverse globalization, which is manifested in geopolitics, economics, in production and work, in environmental and social crises. Various sectors of society articulate, internationally, with the larger objective of achieving a healthy globalization, anchored in an ethic of respect, solidarity, and cooperation, and achieving peace in its various dimensions [military, environmental, social, interior]. One of the important organizations that focuses on this larger objective, the ATTAC group [*Association pour la Taxation des Transactions Financières pour l'Aide aux Citoyens*], recognizes that "Research into alternatives, fortunately already underway, implies, in turn, the local dimension, and political organization on a world scale".[6] This is the starting point for a planetary civilization.

The goal of educational systems, coordinating actions at the local, national, and international levels, should be coherent with the search for new alternatives, not with the reproduction of the current model, anchored in mathematics. As it appears to be inherent to human nature, the new model will also find its support in mathematics, but a new mathematics. The role of a new mathematics in the search for this new economic order is undeniable. It will even be possible to imagine the emergence of "a soft mathematics", as expressed by Keith Devlin[7]; or "an algebra of knowledge", where the transfer of knowledge/practice from one individual to another does not obey the principle of *al-jabr* [transposition] and *al-muqabala* [reduction]. The Program Ethnomathematics, through an alternative reflection on history, philosophy, and education, can contribute to a reformulation of mathematics.

THE UNIVERSALIZATION OF MATHEMATICS

The discipline known as mathematics is an ethnomathematics that originated and developed in Europe, having received some contributions from Indian and Islamic civilizations, and that arrived at its current form in the 16th and 17th Centuries, from which point it began to be carried throughout and imposed upon the rest of the world. Today, this mathematics acquires a character of universality, above all due to the predominance of science and modern technologies which were developed beginning in 17th Century Europe, and which serve to support current economic theories.

The universalization of mathematics was the first step toward the globalization we are witnessing in all activities and areas of knowledge. There used to be much talk about multinationals. Today, the multinationals are, in fact, global companies for which is it impossible to identify a dominant nation or national group.

The idea of globalization began to emerge at the beginning of Christianity and Islam. Unlike Judaism, from which these religions originated, as well as innumerable other beliefs in which there is a chosen people, Christianity and Islam are essentially religions that profess conversion of all humanity to the same faith; of the entire planet subordinated to the same church. This becomes evident in the expansion of the Christianized Roman Empire and of Islam.

The process of globalization of the Christian faith nears its ideal with the great maritime expeditions. The catechism, a fundamental element of conversion, is carried throughout the world. Just as Christianity is a product of the Roman Empire, assuming a universal character with colonialism, so are mathematics, science, and technology.

In the process of expansion, Christianity underwent modifications, absorbing elements of the subordinated culture, and producing remarkable variants of the colonizer's original Christianity. It would be equally expected that the ways of explaining, knowing, coping with, and living with the socio-cultural and natural reality, obviously distinct from region to region, and consequently mathematics, the sciences, and technology, would also undergo this process of "acclimatization", resulting from the cultural dynamic. Nevertheless, this did not happen, and does not happen, and these branches of knowledge acquired an absolute universal character. They do not allow variations nor any kind of relativism. This even became incorporated into the popular saying, "As certain as two plus two is four". The fact that "$2 + 2 = 4$" is not open for discussion, but its contextualization in the form of a symbolic construction that is anchored in an entire cultural history is.

With technology, as well, whose character of response to local conditions is evident, what occurred was a transfer of technology, with slight adaptations.

Mathematics has been conceived of as the science of numbers and forms, of relations and measures, of inferences, and its characteristics point to precision, rigor, exactitude. The great heroes of mathematics, that is, those individuals who are historically pointed to as being responsible for the advancement and consolidation of this science, are identified in Ancient Greece, and later in the Modern Age, in the countries of central Europe, above all England, France, Italy, and Germany. The names most often remembered are Pythagoras, Euclides, Descartes, Galileu, Newton,

Leibniz, Hilbert, Einstein, and Hawkings. They are ideas and men who originated north of the Mediterranean.

The mention of this mathematics and its heroes in diversified cultural groups, such as natives or African Americans, or other non-Europeans in the Americas, groups of oppressed workers and marginalized classes, in general, not only evokes the memory of the conqueror, the slave-holder, ultimately the dominator, but also refers to a way of knowledge that was constructed by him, the dominator, and from which he served himself, and serves himself, to exercise his domination.

Many will say that this is also taking place with "jeans", which are now beginning to substitute all traditional clothing, or with Coca-cola, which is about to replace *guaraná* (the traditional Brazilian soft drink) in Brazil, or with rap music, which is becoming as popular as *samba* in Brazil. However, traditional clothing, *guaraná*, and *samba* continue to be accepted by many Brazilians.

But unlike these cultural manifestations, mathematics has a connotation of infallibility, rigor, and precision, and of being an essential and powerful instrument in the modern world, so that its presence excludes other ways of thinking. In truth, being rational is associated with having a command of mathematics. One even hears talk of mathematism as a doctrine according to which everything happens according to the laws of mathematics. Mathematics presents itself as a wiser god, more miraculous and powerful than the traditional divinities and those of other cultures. If this could be identified as only part of a perverse process of acculturation, through which the essential creativity of being [verb] human is eliminated, we could say that this schooling is a farce. But in truth, it is much worse, because in a farce, once the show is over, everything returns to the way it was. In education, reality is substituted by a false situation, idealized and designed to satisfy the objectives of the dominator. The educational experience falsifies situations with the objective of subordinating. And nothing returns to the real when the experience is over. The cultural roots of the student, which are part of his identity, are eliminated in the process of an educational experience guided by the objective of subordination. This elimination produces a social outcast. These contradictions can be noted in the proposals for "Education for All", the preferred motto of governments and national and international non-governmental organizations in the millennial transition.

The contradictions can be illustrated in the various sectors of society, from the schools for the well-off, to the schools in the poorer neighborhoods, and without forgetting those schools with the objective of "reforming" youth offenders.

The broadest and most dramatic illustration of these contradictions may be the education of indigenous Brazilians. The Indian passes through the educational process and is no longer Indian . . . nor is he White. Without a doubt, the high rate of suicide among the indigenous populations is associated with this.

A natural question may occur following these observations: Would it be better, then, to not teach mathematics to the natives and the marginalized?

This question is applicable to all categories of knowing/doing belonging to the culture of the dominator, in relation to all peoples who present a cultural identity. One could reformulate the question: Would it be better to discourage, or even impede, the popular classes from using jeans, or drinking Coca-cola, or listening to rap music? Naturally, these are false questions, and it would be false and demagogic to respond with a simple "yes" or "no". These questions can only be formulated and answered within an historical context, seeking to understand the evolution of the cultural systems in the history of humanity. If we want to achieve a society with equity and social justice, contextualization is essential for any education program for native and marginal populations, but no less necessary for populations of the dominant sectors.

MATHEMATICS IN CONTEXT

Contextualizing mathematics is essential for everyone. After all, how can one fail to relate Euclides' *Elements* to the cultural panorama of Ancient Greece? Or the adoption of indo-arabic numbers in Europe with the flowering of commerce and trade in the 14th and 15th Centuries? And one cannot understand Newton de-contextualized. It would be possible to repeat some theorems, memorize some tables, and mechanize the execution of operations, and even carry out some derivatives and integrals, which have nothing to do with anything in the cities, in the countryside, or in the forests. Some will say that contextualization is unimportant; that what is important is recognizing mathematics as the noblest manifestation of thought and of human intelligence . . . and in this way, they will justify its importance in the curriculum.

In modern society, intelligence and rationality privilege mathematics. Some even go so far as to say that this construct of Mediterranean thought, taken to its purest form, is the essence of the rational being. And thus it is justified that those who know mathematics have treated, and continue treating, "less rational" individuals, and nature itself, as a bottomless pit for the satisfaction of their desires and ambitions. Mathematics has been an instrument of selection for the elite. [8]

Naturally, there is an important political component to these reflections. Many say that to speak of dominant and subordinate classes is outmoded, left-wing jargon, but no one can deny that this distinction between classes continues to exist, in the central as well as the peripheral countries.

It is fitting, therefore, to refer to a "dominant mathematics", which is an instrument developed by the central countries and often used as an instrument of domination. This mathematics, and those who have a command of it, present a superior posture, with the power to displace, or even eliminate, the mathematics of the "everyday". The same occurs with other cultural forms. Particularly interesting are Basil Bernstein's studies of language. [9] Also well-studied are situations related to behavior, medicine, art, and religion. All of these manifestations are referred to as popular culture. Naturally, despite being alive and practiced, popular culture is often ignored, disparaged, rejected, repressed. Certainly its importance is diminished. The effect is to discourage, and even eliminate, the people as producers of culture, and consequently, as a cultural entity.

This is no less true with mathematics. In geometry and arithmetic in particular, violent contradictions can be noted.

For example, the geometry of the people, exemplified by the miniature hot air balloons and the kites that they construct, is colorful. Theoretical geometry, since its Greek origin, eliminated color. Many readers at this point will be confused. They will be saying, "But what does this have to do with anything? Kites and balloons? Colors?" It has everything to do with it, as these are precisely the first and most remarkable geometrical experiences. [10] And the re-approximation of art and geometry cannot be achieved without the mediation of color.

In arithmetic, the attribute, i.e., the quality of the number in the quantification is essential. Two oranges and two horses are distinct "two's". To arrive at the abstract "two", without a qualifier, like arriving at a geometry without colors, is perhaps the crucial point in the passage from mathematics of the concrete to theoretical mathematics.

Taking care with this passage, and handling this moment appropriately, may synthesize the most important objective of elementary mathematics programs. The others are techniques which, little by little, as the young person accumulates other experiences, become interesting and necessary. Care with this passage from the concrete to the abstract is one of the methodological characteristics of ethnomathematics.

One cannot define criteria of superiority among cultural manifestations. Properly contextualized, no cultural form can be said to be superior to another. In her important book about indigenous mathematics, Mariana Kawall Leal Ferreira shows how the binary system of the *xavantes* was substituted, as if by magic, by a "more efficient" base-10 system.[11] Why more efficient? Does it relate to the context of the *xavante*? No, but it relates to the numeration of the dominator. What happens with the native religion, native food habits and native language is no different.

Without a doubt, there is a utilitarian criterion in education and in intercultural relations. Without learning the "White man's mathematics", the Indian will be fooled in their commercial transactions with the White man[12]; just as, without covering up his nudity, and without having a command of the White man's language, it will be difficult for the Indian to have access to the dominant society. But this occurs in all cultures. I must have a command of English to participate in the international academic world. And, when participating in a dissertation defense or qualifying examination in a traditional university, I must wear a magistrate's robe! Yet no one ever said or insinuated that it would be good for me to forget Portuguese, and that I should feel shy, or even ashamed, about speaking this language, or that the clothing that I use every day among my peers could lead me into the circle of the indecent in hell.

But this is what is done with many peoples, especially with indigenous peoples. Their nudity is indecent and sinful, their language is considered useless, their religion is labeled "superstition", and their mathematics is "imprecise", "inefficient", and "useless", if not "nonexistent". The same occurs in exactly the same manner with the poorer social classes, even non-Indians.

61

This is exactly what happens with a child, with an adolescent, or even with an adult, when they go to school. One escape for Indians has been suicide. In general, in the encounter with the dominant classes, principally in the schools, a different form of suicide is practiced; a suicide that is manifested in a deep internal emptiness, drug use, and violence, revealing an attitude of disbelief and alienation, so well-portrayed in the films *Kids* and *American Beauty*. Nihilism is one of the striking characteristics of today's society.

THE ENCOUNTER OF CULTURES

The encounter of cultures is a fact that is as much a part of human relations as the phenomenon of life itself. There is no encounter with another without the manifestation of a cultural dynamic. In the colonial period, as was the case of Brazil, this dynamic was resolved through educational systems with explicit objectives of domination and subordination. The colonial system of education is perverse.

We have arrived at a structure of society, at perverse concepts of culture, of nation and sovereignty, that impose the convenience and even the necessity of teaching language, mathematics, medicine, the laws of the dominator to the dominated, whether Indian or White, rich or poor, children or adults. What must be questioned is the aggression to the dignity and cultural identity of those who are subordinated to this structure. A greater responsibility of educational theorists is to warn about the irreversible damage that can be caused to a culture, to a people, and to an individual, if the process is carried out recklessly, often even with good intentions, and to offer proposals to minimize this damage.

The majority of educators do not have the perverse attitude mentioned above. However, many educators are unfortunately naive about coping with the cultural dynamic; and the consequences of naivete and perversity are essentially no different.

Referring still to indigenous education, it is possible to avoid cultural conflicts that result from the introduction of the "White man's mathematics" in indigenous education; for example, by dealing appropriately with the formulation and resolution of simple arithmetic problems. Various examples, such as boat transportation, management of bank accounts, and others, show that the indigenous peoples have a command of what is essential for their practices and to elaborate argumentation with the Whites about that which is of interest to them, normally focussed on transportation, commerce, or land use.

Contextualized mathematics presents itself as one more resource for resolving new problems that, having originated from the other culture, arrive demanding the intellectual instruments of that other culture. The ethnomathematics of the White man is useful for these new problems, and it cannot be ignored. The ethnomathematics of the community is useful, efficient and appropriate for many other things belonging to its culture, to that *ethno*, and there is no reason to substitute it. Claiming that one is more efficient, more rigorous, ultimately better that the other is a question that, if removed from the context, is false and falsifying.

The greater objective of the educator's intervention is to perfect practices and reflections and instruments of critique. This process of perfecting occurs not as an imposition, but as an option. As Eduardo Sebastiani Ferreira said, "It is up to the community to decide; it can accept these results or not." [13]

The domain of two ethnomathematics, and possibly of others, offers greater possibilities for explaining, understanding, handling new situations and resolving problems. But this is exactly how good mathematical research is done – and, in truth, research in any other field of knowledge. The access to a larger number of materials and intellectual instruments, when properly contextualized, gives greater capacity to face situations and resolve new problems, to appropriately model a real situation in order to, with these instruments, arrive at a possible solution or course of action.

The capacity to explain, learn and comprehend, to critically face new situations, constitutes learning *par excellence*. Learning is not the simple acquisition of techniques and abilities, nor the memorization of a few explanations and theories.

Formal education, based on the transmission of explanations and theories using a lecture format, and training in techniques and skills (practical teaching using repetitive exercises) is entirely mistaken, as shown by more recent advances in our understanding of cognitive processes. Cognitive skills cannot be evaluated outside of the cultural context. Obviously, cognitive ability is proper to each individual. There are cognitive styles that should be recognized between distinct cultures, in the intercultural context, as well as within the same culture, in the intracultural context.

Each individual organizes their intellectual process over the length of their life history. Advances in meta-cognition make it possible to understand this process. However, when attempting to "compatibilize" the intellectual organizations of individuals in order to, in this way, create a socially acceptable framework, the authenticity and individuality of each of the participants in this process must not be eliminated. The great challenge one encounters in education is precisely to enable the learner to interpret the abilities and the cognitive action itself of each individual, not in the linear, stable, continuous fashion which is characteristic of the more commonly used educational practices.

The fragility of pedagogical structuralism, anchored in what we call the myths of current education, is evident when we note the vertiginous drop in educational results anchored in these myths; and this is true throughout the world. The alternative that we propose is to recognize that each individual is an integral and integrated whole, and that their cognitive and organizing practices are not disassociated from the historical context in which the process occurs – a context with is permanently evolving. This is evident in the dynamic that characterizes Good Education for All: education of the masses.

The adoption of a new educational posture, in truth the search for a new paradigm of education that substitutes the worn-out teaching-learning, based on an obsolete cause-effect relation, is essential for developing creativity that is uninhibited and leads to new forms of intercultural relations, providing the appropriate space for preserving diversity and eliminating inequality in a new organization of society.

As I already mentioned above, we are living in a changing civilization, which affects all our behavior, values, and actions, education in particular.

I understand mathematics as a strategy developed by the human species throughout its history to explain, understand, deal with and live with the sensible, perceivable world, and with the imaginary world, naturally within a natural and cultural context. The same occurs with the techniques, the arts, the religions and sciences in general. It is about the construction of bodies of knowledge in total symbiosis within the same temporal and spatial context, which have obviously varied according to the geography and history of the individuals and the various cultural groups to which they belong – families, tribes, societies, civilizations. The greater end of these bodies of knowledge has been the will, which is essentially a necessity, of these cultural groups to survive in their environment and transcend, spatially and temporally, this environment.

Education is a strategy to stimulate the individual and collective development generated by these same cultural groups toward the end of maintaining themselves as they are and advancing in the satisfaction of these needs to survive and transcend.

Consequently, mathematics and education are strategies that are contextualized and interdependent. In this book, I have reflected on the evolution of both, and analyzed the trends as I see them in the current state of civilization. I see no greater priority than achieving peace in its various dimensions.

THE VARIOUS DIMENSIONS OF PEACE

In the current state of civilization, it is fundamental to focus on our actions, as individuals, as a society, in the realization of an ideal of Education for Peace and a for a happy humanity.

When I speak of Education for Peace, many come with the question, "But what does this have to do with mathematics education?", and I respond, "It has everything to do with it." [14]

I could synthesize my position, saying that one can only justify insistence on "Education for All" if it were possible to obtain, through it, a better quality of life and greater dignity for humanity as a whole. The dignity of each individual is manifested in the encounter of each individual with others. Thus, achieving a state of inner peace is a priority. [15] Many are still asking, "What does this have to do with mathematics education?", and I insist on saying, "It has everything to do with it".

Achieving a state of inner peace is difficult, above all due to all the problems we face in our daily lives, particularly in our relationship with the other. Could it be that the other also finds it difficult to achieve a state of inner peace? Without a doubt, the state of inner peace can be affected by material difficulties, such as the lack of security, lack of employment, lack of a salary, and often even the lack of housing or food. Social peace is a state in which these difficulties do not present themselves. Solidarity with our fellow man to overcome these difficulties is a first manifestation in order for us to feel part of society and move toward social peace. And for certain the question again arises: "But what does mathematics have to do with this?" It is not for me to give another answer to those mathematicians who fail to perceive how this is all related. I suggest a broad vision of the history of humanity and of the history of ideas to perceive that mathematics has everything to do with this.

Few also understand that environmental peace has to do with mathematics, which is always thought of as applied to development and progress. I remember that modern science, which rests largely on mathematics, gives is remarkable instruments for a good relationship with nature, but powerful instruments to destroy this same nature, as well.[16]

The multiple dimensions of peace [inner peace, social peace, environmental peace, and military peace] are the first objects of any educational system. The greatest justification for efforts for scientific and technological advancement is to achieve total peace, and, as such, it should be the substrate of every planning discourse.

This should be the dream of the human being. I remember what the two eminent mathematicians, Albert Einstein and Bertrand Russell, said in the Pugwash Manifesto of 1955: "Forget everything and remember humanity." I seek, in my proposals for mathematics education, to follow the teachings of these two great masters, from whom I learned a great deal of mathematics, and above all, learned about humanity. My proposal is to fashion Education for Peace, and in particular, Mathematics Education for Peace.

Many will continue to be intrigued: "But how does one relate 2nd degree trinomials to peace?" It is likely that these same individuals are accustomed to teaching the 2nd degree trinomial by giving, as an example, a trajectory of a cannon ball shot from a cannon. But I am almost certain that they do not say, nor even suggest, that that beautiful mathematical instrumental, the 2nd degree trinomial, is what gives certain individuals – the professional artillerists, who were probably the best students in their mathematics class – the capacity to shoot a deadly bomb from a cannon to reach a population of people, of human beings, flesh and bones, emotions and desires, and kill them, destroy their homes and temples, destroy trees and animals nearby, pollute any lake or river in the surroundings. The implicit message ends up being: Learn the 2nd degree trinomial well, and you will be able to do this. Only he who completes a good mathematics course has a sufficient theoretical base to point cannons at populations.

Of course, my opponents will say, as they have already said, "But this is a demagogic discourse. This horrific destruction will be done only when necessary, and it is important that our youth be prepared for what is necessary". And my content-oriented colleagues say, as a last resort, the following: "It is necessary to possess and know well the material and intellectual instruments of the enemy to be able to defeat him." Such thinking gave support to the doctrine of discouragement [arm yourselves to the teeth to discourage potential enemies], responsible for the unbridled military expansion in the so-called Cold War. During the Cold War, millions were illuded by this simplistic and false doctrine, with material and moral losses to all of humanity.

It is important to remember that those who have a stake in this state of affairs justify it by saying that it is necessary because we will be the targets of individuals who do not profess the same religious creed, are not of the same political party, do not follow our economic model of property and production, do not have our same color of skin or our language; ultimately, we are the object of the destructive intent of the other, who is different. This is because it is believed that the different is, potentially, our enemy, interested in our elimination. This has been, and continues to be, the favorite argument used by those who are in power to, in this way, maintain themselves in power. This argument permeates social and political proposals.

This discourse derived from my example of the 2nd degree trinomial. I drew attention to a very ugly consequence of something as lovely as the 2nd degree trinomial. I am not proposing to eliminate the 2nd degree trinomial from programs, but rather that some time be taken to show, critically, the ugly things that are done with it, and to highlight the beautiful things that can be done with it.

Total peace essentially depends on each individual knowing himself and being integrated into his society, into humanity, nature, and the cosmos. Throughout each or our existence, we can learn mathematics, but we cannot lose the knowledge of ourselves, nor create barriers between individuals and others, between individuals and society, and generate habits of mistrust of the other, of disbelief in society, of disrespect and ignorance of humanity, which is one, of nature which is common to all, and the universe as a whole.

How do I see myself as a mathematics educator? I see myself as an educator whose field of ability and competence is mathematics, and who uses it, but not as a mathematician who uses his position as an educator to impart and transmit his mathematical abilities and competencies. My science and my knowledge are subordinated to my humanism. As a mathematics educator, I seek to utilize what I have learned as a mathematician to realize my mission as an educator. In very clear and direct terms: the student is more important than programs and content. Spreading this message is my aim as a teacher of teachers.

Knowledge is the most important strategy to lead the individual to being at peace with herself and with her social, cultural, and natural surroundings, and to situate herself in a cosmic reality.

There is, effectively, a morality that is intrinsic to knowledge, and in particular, to mathematical knowledge. Why insist on education and mathematics education, and on doing mathematics itself, if we do not perceive how our practice can help to achieve a new organization of society, a planetary civilization anchored in respect, solidarity, and cooperation?

Achieving this new organization of society is my utopia. As an educator, I seek to orient my actions in this direction, however utopic. How to be an educator without having a utopia?

APPENDIX

THESES AND DISSERTATIONS ON ETHNOMATHEMATICS IN BRAZIL

Innumberable theses and dissertations have been defended in Brazil and other countries with ethnomathematics as their focus. Some have been mentioned in the preceding chapters.

The data bank organized by Dario Fiorentini, of CEMPEM, Faculdade de Educação da UNICAMP, most closely approximates a complete account in Brazil. The *Compendium - Newsletter of the ISGEm* reports on those presented at universities outside Brazil. It would be nearly impossible to make a complete account of all the theses and dissertations, even those just in Brazil.

The efforts of Mônica Rabelo in helping to collect this information must be mentioned. With the collaboration of Maria do Carmo Domite, coordinator of the *Grupo de Estudos e Pesquisa em Etnomatemática* (GEPEm), of the Faculdade de Educação da Universidade de São Paulo, and of Mary Lúcia Guimarães Pedro and Andréia Lunkes Conrado, both members of this group, it was possible to gather abstracts, in Portuguese and English, of the theses and dissertations defended in Brazilian universities, and publish them as a collection in a book entitled *Pesquisa em Etnomatemática*, Faculdade de Ciências e Tecnologia da Universidade Nova de Lisboa, 2002, also available on the site: http://www.fe.unb.br/etnomatematica/resumosdeteses.htm. The following theses and dissertations are described, including the abstract, institution, advisor, year:

Acioly-Regnier, Nadja Maria: *A lógica matemática do jogo do bicho: compreensão ou utilização de regras?*
Borba, Marcelo de Carvalho: *Um estudo de etnomatemática: sua incorporação na elaboração de uma proposta pedagógica para o núcleo - escola da favela da Vila Nogueira - São Quirino.*
Abreu, Guida Maria Correia Pinto de: *O uso da matemática na agricultura: o caso dos produtores de cana-de-açúcar.*
Grando, Neiva Ignês: *A matemática na agricultura e na escola.*

Buriasco, Regina Luzia Corio de: *Matemática de fora e de dentro da escola: do bloqueio à transição.*

Souza, Angela Calazans: *Educação matemática na alfabetização de adultos e adolescentes segundo a proposta pedagógica de Paulo Freire.*

Nobre, Sérgio: *Aspectos Sociais e Culturais no Desenho Curricular da Matemática.*

Carvalho, Nelson L. C.: *Etnomatemática: o conhecimento matemático que se constrói na resistência cultural.*

Caldeira, Ademir Donizeti: *Uma proposta pedagógica em etnomatemática na zona rural da Fazenda Angélica em Rio Claro - São Paulo.*

Pompeu, Geraldo: *Trazendo a Etnomatemática para o Currículo escolar: Uma investigação das atitudes dos professores e da aprendizagem dos alunos.*

Ferreira, Mariana Kawall Leal: *Da Origem dos homens à conquista da escrita: um estudo sobre povos indígenas e educação escolar no Brasil.*

Clareto, Sonia Maria: *A Criança e seus Mundos: Céu, Terra e Mar no olhar de crianças da comunidade caiçara de Camburi (SP).*

Costa, Wanderleya Nara Gonçalves: *Os ceramistas do Vale do Jequitinhonha.*

Neeleman, Willem: *Ensino de Matemática em Moçambique e sua relação com a cultura "tradicional".*

Abreu, Guida Maria Correia Pinto de: *A relação entre a matemática de casa e da escola numa comunidade rural no Brasil.*

Acioly-Regnier, Nadja Maria: *A justa medida : um estudo das competências matemáticas de trabalhadores da cana de açúcar do nordeste do Brasil no domínio da medida.*

Knijnik, Gelsa: *Matemática, Educação e Cultura na luta pela terra.*

Mendes, Jackeline Rodrigues: *Descompassos na interação Professor-Aluno na aula de matemática em contexto indígena.*

Bello, Samuel Edmundo López: *Educação Matemática Indígena: um estudo etnomatemático com os índios Guarani-Kaiova do Mato Grosso do Sul.*

Marafon, Adriana César de Mattos: *A influência da família na aprendizagem da Matemática.*

Freitas, Franceli Fernandes de: *A formação de professoras da Ilha de Maré – Bahia.*

Scandiuzzi, Pedro Paulo: *A dinâmica da contagem de Lahatua Otomo e suas implicações educacionais: uma pesquisa em etnomatemática.*

Monteiro, Alexandrina: *Etnomatemática: as possibilidades pedagógicas num curso de alfabetização para trabalhadores rurais assentados.*

Oliveira, Cláudio José de: *Matemática escolar e práticas sociais no cotidiano da vila Fátima: um estudo etnomatemático.*

Grando, Neiva Ignês: *O campo conceitual de espaço na escola e em outros contextos culturais.*

Amancio, Chateaubriand Nunes: *Os Kanhgág da bacia do Tibagi: Um estudo etnomatemático em comunidades indígenas.*

Anastácio, Maria Queiroga Amoroso: *Três ensaios numa articulação sobre a racionalidade, o corpo e a educação na Matemática.*

Oliveira, Helena Dória Lucas de: *Atividades Produtivas do Campo, Etnomatemática e a Educação do Movimento Sem Terra.*

Scandiuzzi, Pedro Paulo: *Educação Indígena X Educação Escolar Indígena: uma relação etnocida em uma pesquisa etnomatemática.*

Bello, Samuel Edmundo López: *Etnomatemática: relações e tensões entre as distintas formas de explicar e conhecer.*

Halmenschlager, Vera Lúcia da S.: *Etnia, raça e desigualdade educacional: Uma abordagem etnomatemática no ensino médio noturno.*

Marafon, Adriana César de Mattos: *Vocação Matemática como Reconecimento Académico.*

Oliveira, Cristiane Coppe de: *Do Menino "Julinho" à "Malba Tahan": Uma viagem pelo Oásis do Ensino da Matemática.*

Wanderer, Fernanda: *Educação de Jovens e Adultos e produtos da mídia: possibilidades de um processo pedagógico etnomatemático.*

Giongo, Ieda Maria: *Educação e produção do calçado em tempos de globalização: um estudo etnomatemático.*

Mendes, Jackeline Rodrigues: *Ler, Escrever e Contar: Práticas de Numeramento-Letramento dos Kaiabi no Contexto de Formação de Professores Índios do Parque Indígena do Xingu.*

Vianna, Márcio de Albuquerque: *A escola da Matemática e a escola do samba: um estudo etnomatemático pela valorização da cultura popular no ato cognitivo.*

Schmitz, Carmen Cecília: *Caracterizando a matemática escolar: um estudo na Escola Bom Fim.*

Bandeira, Francisco de Assis: *A cultura de hortaliças e a cultura matemática em Gramorezinho: uma fertilidade sociocultural.*

Junior, Gilberto Chieus: *Matemática caiçara: Etnomatemática contribuindo na formação docente.*

Lucena, Isabel Cristina Rodrigues de: *Carpinteiros Navais de Abaetetuba: etnomatemática navega rios da Amazônia.*

CHAPTER 1. WHY ETHNOMATHEMATICS?

[1] Ubiratan D'Ambrosio: "A matemática na época das grandes navegações e início da colonização", *Revista Brasileira de História da Matemática*, v.1, n.1, 2001.

[2] An interesting study of the presence of the New World in the literature, with a focus on scientific knowledge, is Denise Albanese's book: *New Science, New World*, Duke University Press, Durham, 1996.

[3] Antonello Gerbi: *O novo mundo. História de uma polêmica (1750–1900)*, translated by. Bernardo Joffily (orig.1996), Companhia das Letras, São Paulo, 1996.

[4] Alexander von Humboldt: *Cosmos. A Sketch of the Physical Description of the Universe*, 2 vols., tr. E.C. Otté (1858; orig. 1845–1862), The Johns Hopkins University Press, Baltimore, 1997; v.1, p. 36. This book was a *best-seller* when it was published.

[5] *op.cit.*; p.37.

[6] Oswald Spengler: *A decadência do Ocidente. Esboço de uma morfologia da História Universal*, condensed edition by Helmut Werner, translated by Herbert Caro (orig. 1959), Zahar Editores, Rio de Janeiro, 1973; p.68.

[7] It is worth remembering that Johann Wolfgang von Goethe (1749–1832), considered to be the first great Romanticist writer and a great German poet, was a noted scientist, but was totally opposed to the ideas of Newton. In education, Goethe was, in the transition from the 19th to the 20th Centuries, the great inspiration for Rudolf Steiner (1861–1925), the founder of Anthroposophy and proponent of Waldorf education.

[8] Y.Akizuki: Proposal to I.C.M.I., *L'Enseignement mathématique*, t.V, fasc.4, 1960; pp. 288–289.

[9] The correspondence between Lakatos and Feyerabend shows the vacillations, and even contraditions, that ravaged the philosophical sphere as a result of the polarization of positions. See Imre Lakatos and Paul Feyerabend: *For and Against Method: Including Lakato's Lectures on Scientific Method and the Lakatos-Feyerabend Correspondence*. Edited and with an introduction by Matteo Motterlini, The University of Chicago Press, Chicago, 1999.

[10] Care should be taken not to be taken in by the epistemological and methodological limitations of the new "interdisciplinary" disciplines, which, as we see with the history of science, foreshadowed disciplines that are common in school curricula today. Characterizing ethnomathematics as an interdisciplinary field is limiting.

[11] My historiographical proposal, which is heavily influenced by Oswald Spengler, approximates that proposed by Marc Bloch and Lucien Febvre in *Annales.* See Ubiratan D'Ambrosio: *"A Historiographical Proposal for Non-western Mathematics, in Helaine Selin"*, ed.: *Mathematics Across Cultures. The History of Non-western Mathematics,* Kluwer Academic Publishers, Dordrecht, 2000; pp. 79–92.

[12] An interesting study about the cultural dynamic, albeit restricted to the West, is the book by Francesco Alberoni: *Gênese. Como se criam os mitos, os valores e as instituições da civilização ocidental,* translated by Mario Fondelli, Rocco, Rio de Janeiro, 1991 (orig. ed. 1989).

[13] I recommend the film/videa *Quest for Fire*, dir: Jean-Jacques Annaud, 1982.

[14] William H. McNeill: *"Passing Strange: The Convergence of Evolutionary Science with Scientific History"*, *History and Theory,* vol. 40, n°1, February 2001; pp. 1–15.

[15] A classic is the book by Luis da Câmara Cascudo: *História da alimentação no Brasil*, Coleção Brasiliana, São Paulo, 1967. Also very interesting are the studies in the book by Jean-Louis Flandrin and Massimo Montanari (orgs.): História da Alimentação, translated by Luciano Vieira Machado and Guilherme João de Freitas Teixeira, 2nd edition, Estação Liberdade, São Paulo, 1998 (orig. ed.1996). See, in particular, Chapter 1: As estratégias alimentares nos tempos pré-históricos, by Catherine Perlès, pp. 36–53. Unfortunately, the book is entirely focused on Europe. About Latin America, we have the books by Eduardo Estrella: *El Pan de América. Etnohistória de los Alimentos Aborígenes em el Ecuador*, Centro de Estúdios Históricos, Madrid, 1986; Teresa Rojas Rabiela/William T. Sanders: *Historia de la agricultura. Época prehispanica – siglo XVI*, Instituto Nacional de Antropologia e Historia, Mexico, 1985.

[16] See the fascinating book by Jean Marcale: *La grande déesse: Mythes et sanctuaires*, Editions Albin Michel, Paris, 1997.

[17] This is the story, told in the Bible (Genesis 41), of the pharaoh's dream about the seven cows and seven ears of grain which the

pharaoh calls Joseph to interpret. The consequence is one of the first manifestations of science used in social organization. Joseph, the wise man, suddenly raised to a position of power, organizes the systems of production, harvest, and storage, avoiding hunger in the Pharaoh's domains. The idea of the distribution of land and payment of taxes is found in Herôdotos: *História*, translated by Mário da Gama Kury, Editora Universidade de Brasília, Brasília, 1985; p. 121.

[18] An excellent book is E.G.Richards: *Mapping Time. The Calendar and Its History*, Oxford University Press, Oxford, 1998.

[19] José Carlos Borsato: *Uma experiência de integração curricular: Projeto Áreas Verdes*, Masters Thesis in Mathematics and Science Education, UNICAMP/OEA/MEC, 1984. See the summary in Ubiratan D'Ambrosio (org.): *O ensino de Ciências e Matemática na América Latina*, Editora da UNICAMP/Papirus Editora, Campinas, 1984; pp. 202–203.

[20] Gelsa Knijnik: *Exclusão e resistência. Educação Matemática e legitimidade cultural*, Artes Médicas, Porto Alegre, 1996.

[21] Alexandrina Monteiro: *Etnomatemática: as possibilidades pedagógicas num curso de alfabetização para trabalhadores rurais assentados*, Doctoral dissertation, Faculdade de Educação da UNICAMP, Campinas, 1998.

[22] Maria Luisa Oliveras: *Etnomatemáticas en Trabajos de Artesania Andaluza. Su Integración en un Modelo para la Formación de Profesores y en la Innovación del Currículo Matemático Escolar*, Doctoral dissertation, Universidad de Granada, Espanha, 1995; *Etnomatemáticas. Formación de profesores e innovación curricular*, Editorial Comares, Granada, 1996.

[23] Terezinha Carraher, David Carraher, Analúcia Schliemann: *Na vida dez, na escola zero*, Cortez Editora, São Paulo, 1988. Regina Luzia Corio de Buriasco: *Matemática de fora e de dentro da escola: do Bloqueio à Transição*, Dissertação de Mestrado, Instituto de Geociências e Ciências Exatas da UNESP, Rio Claro, 1989.

[24] Marilyn Frankenstein: *Relearning Mathematics. A Different Third R – Radical Mathematics*, Free Association Books, London, 1989.

[25] Cinzia Bonotto: Sull'uso di artefatti culturali nell'insegnamento-apprendimento della matematica/About the use of cultural artifacts in the teaching-learning of mathematics, *L'Educazione Matematica*, Anno XX, Serie VI,1(2),1999; pp. 62–95.

[26] Adriana César de Mattos Marafon: *A influência da família na aprendizagem da matemática*, Masters thesis, Instituto de Geociências e Ciências Exatas, UNESP, Rio Claro, 1996.

[27] Tod L. Shockey: *The Mathematical Behavior of a Group of Thoracic Cardiovascular Surgeons*, Ph.D. Dissertation, Curry School of Education, University of Virginia, Charlottsville, USA, 1999.

[28] Maria do Carmo Villa: *Conceptions manifestées par les élèves dans une épreuve de simulation d'une situation aléatoire réalisée au moyen d'um matériel concret*, Tèse de Doctorat, Faculte dês Sciences de l'Université Laval, Québec, Canadá, 1993.

[29] N.M.Acioly: *A lógica do jogo do bicho: compreensão ou utilização de regras?* (Masters thesis), Recife: Universidade Federal de Pernambuco, Programa de Psicologia Cognitiva, 1985. Sergio R. Nobre: *Aspectos sociais e culturais no desenho curricular da matemática*, Masters thesis, Instituto de Geociências e Ciências Exatas, UNESP, Rio Claro, 1989.

[30] Malba Tahan: *O Jogo do Bicho à luz da Matemática*, Grafipar Editora, Curitiba, n/d [after 1975].

[31] Marcelo de Carvalho Borba: *Um estudo de Etnomatemática: Sua incorporação na elaboração de uma proposta pedagógica para o Núcleo Escola da favela da Vila Nogueira/São Quirino*, Masters thesis, Instituto de Geociências e Ciências Exatas, UNESP, Rio Claro, 1987.

[32] Wilhelm Neeleman: *Ensino de Matemática em Moçambique e sua relação com a cultura tradicional*, Masters thesis, Instituto de Geociências e Ciências Exatas, UNESP, 1993.

[33] One can see see how to use this pedagogical resource by reading the article by Anthony C. Stevens, Janet M. Sharp, and Becky Nelson: *"The Intersection of Two Unlikely Worlds: Ratios and Drums"*, *Teaching Children Mathematics* (NCTM), vol. 7, n°6, February 2001; pp. 376–383.

[34] Claudia Zaslavsky: *Africa Counts. Number and Pattern in African Cultures*, Third Edition, Lawrence Hill Books, Chicago, 1999 (1st edition 1973).

[35] Paulus Gerdes: *Sobre o despertar do pensamento geométrico*, Editora da UFPR, Curitiba, 1992.

[36] A basic reference is the book by Michael P. Closs, ed.: *Native Americans Mathematics*, University of Texas Press, Austin, 1986. One cannot forget to mention the pioneering book by Márcia and Robert Ascher: *Code of the Quipus: A study in media, mathematics and culture*, University of Michigan Press, Ann Arbor, 1981.

[37] Samuel López Bello: Etnomatemática: *Relações e tensões entre as distintas formas de explicar e conhecer*, Doctoral dissertation, Faculdade de Educação da UNICAMP, Campinas, 2000.

[38] This theme was discussed by Chateaubriand Nunes Amâncio: *Os Kanhgág da Bacia do Tibagi: Um estudo etnomatemático em comunidades indígenas*, Masters thesis, Instituto de Geociências e Ciências Exatas, UNESP, Rio Claro, 1999.

CHAPTER 2. THE VARIOUS DIMENSIONS OF ETHNOMATHEMATICS

[1] See the article by Osmo Pekonen: *"Gerbert of Aurillac: Mathematician and Pope"*, The Mathematical Intelligencer, vol. 22, n.4, 2000; pp. 67−70.

[2] Frei Vicente do Salvador: *História do Brasil 1500−1627*, Journal by Capistrano de Abreu, Rodolfo Garcia and Frei Venâncio Willeke, OFM, Edições Melhoramentos, São Paulo, 1965.

[3] Oliver Sacks: *Um antropólogo em Marte. Sete histórias paradoxais*, translation by Bernardo Carvalho, Companhia das Letras, São Paulo, 1995.

[4] See the book by Brian Butterworth: *What Counts. How Every Brain Is Hardwired for Math*, The Free Press, New York, 1999.

[5] The recent book by Daniel J. Povinelli, *Folk Physics for Apes. The Chimpanzee's Theory of How the World Works*, Oxford University Press, Oxford, 2000, provoked considerable controversy. Without a doubt, it is a field of very active research.

[6] See Juyang Weng et al., *"Autonomous Mental Development by Robots and Machines"*, Science, vol. 291, 26 January 2001; pp. 599−600.

[7] A good synthesis of the pre-history of mathematics is the book by Manoel de Campos Almeida: *Origens da Matemática*, Editora Universitária Champagnat, Curitiba, 1998.

[8] Ubiratan D'Ambrosio: *Several Dimensions of Science Education. A Latin American Perspective*, CIDE/REDUC, Santiago, 1990.

[9] Ron Eglash: *"Anthropological Perspectives on Ethnomathematics"*, in Selin, Helaine, ed.: *Mathematics Across Cultures. The History of Non-Western Mathematics*, Kluwer Academic Publishers, Dordrecht, 2000; pp. 13−22.

[10] Ubiratan D'Ambrosio: *"The cultural dynamics of the encounter of two worlds after 1492 as seen in the development of scientific thought"*, Impact of Science on Society, n. 167, vol. 42/3, 1992; pp. 205–214.

[11] Co-optation is the cruelest form of domination. The co-opted man was the *"capitão-do-mato"* (escaped slave hunter) in the history of slavery, and the award-winning worker symbolized in the film *O homem que virou suco*, by João Batista de Andrade (1981), will be the *blade-runner* of the future. The most dramatic and transparent denunciation of the co-optation practiced during colonialism is the character in *Gunga Din*, from a poem by Rudyard Kipling, which gave origin to the film of the same name, directed by Georges Stevens (1939).

[12] An excellent study of the preservation of African traditions in Brazil is found in the video *Atlântico Negro – Nas rotas dos Orixás*, a documentary by Renato Barbieri, Videografia Criação e Produção, 1998.

[13] Illustrative of this domination of the quantitative over the qualitative is the change in the name of the discipline most central to modern thought, from Analysis to Calculus, which occurred in the 19th Century.

[14] See the interesting article by Anthony Ralston: *"Let's Abolish Pencil-and-Paper Arithmetic"*, Journal of Computers in Mathematics and Science Teaching, v.18, n. 2, 1999; pp. 173–194.

[15] An example of how these modern, advanced theories can be related to ethnomathematics can be found in the book by Ron Eglash: *African Fractals. Modern Computing and Indigenous Design*, Rutgers University Press, New Brunswick, 1999.

[16] The communicative, analytical, and material instruments, called *literacy, matheracy,* and *technoracy*, are discussed in my book *Educação para uma sociedade em transição*, Papirus Editora, Campinas, 1999.

[17] Beatriz Silva D'Ambrosio: Formação de Professores de Matemática para o Século XXI: o Grande Desafio, *Pro-Posições*, v. 4, n.1[10], March 1993, p. 35-41; p. 39.

[18] Teresa Vergani: *Educação Etnomatemática: O que é?*, Pandora Edições, Lisboa, 2000; p. 12.

CHAPTER 3. KNOWLEDGE AND BEHAVIOR

[1] The undeniable importance of Lev Vygotsky and Jean Piaget, when they based their learning theories on careful direct observations of subjects in their own environment, does not justify the continuing domination of their theories in psychology courses in teacher education programs. An excellent synthesis of current psychology, focusing on the child's first years of life, is the book by Alison Gopnik, Andrew N.Meltzoff and Patrícia K.Kuhl: *The Scientist in the Crib. Minds, Brains, and How Children Learn*, William Morrow and Company, Inc., New York, 1999.

[2] See Sergio Carlos Covello: *Comenius. A construção da pedagogia*. Editora Comenius, São Paulo, 1999.

[3] The present is a philosophical question of the same nature as the irrational, which has dominated philosophy since the times of Ancient Greece.

[4] Oliver Sacks: *Um antropólogo em Marte. Sete histórias paradoxais*, translation by Bernardo Carvalho. Companhia das Letras, São Paulo, 1995; pp.141−142.

[5] Humberto Maturana: *"The Effectiveness of Mathematical Formalisms"*, *Cybernetics & Human Knowing*, vol. 7, n°2-3, 2000, pp. 147−150.

[6] Claudia Dreifus: *"Do Androids Dream? M.I.T. Is Working on It (A Conversation with Anne Foerst)"*, *The New York Times*, November 7, 2000.

[7] Anthony Ralston: *"Let's Abolish Pencil-and-Paper Arithmetic"*, *Journal of Computers in Mathematics and Science Teaching*, vol. 18, n°2, 1999; pp. 173−194.

[8] Ron Eglash: *African Fractals. Modern Computing and Indigenous Design*, Rutgers University Press, New Brunswick, 1999.

[9] Ubiratan D'Ambrosio: Teoria das catástrofes: Um estudo em sociologia da ciência, *THOT. Uma publicação transdisciplinar da Associação Palas Athena*, n°67, 1997; pp. 38−48.

[10] The beginning of time, as it appears in systems of explanation.

[11] Seethe book by Mario Alighiero Manacorda: *História da Educação. Da Antiguidade aos nossos dias*, trad. Gaetano Lo Monaco, Cortez Editora, São Paulo, 1996.. The greatest question in the search for explanations. From the book of Genesis to the Big Bang theory, myths of creation constitute the basis for all the explanations.

[12] J.A. Comério: *Didáctica Magna. Tratado da Arte Universal de Ensinar Tudo a Todos* [orig.edition. 1656], Introduction, translation, and notes by Joaquim Ferreira Gomes, Fundação Calouste Gulbenkian, 1966; p.71.

[13]Translator's note: in the original Portuguese text, the author used the word *inidônio*, i.e. the opposite of *idônio:* appropriate for something, apt, capable, competent.. The translation for *inidônio* used in the text was inept.

[14] Ubiratan D'Ambrosio: *Educação para uma Sociedade em Transição*, Papirus Editora, Campinas, 1999.

[15] To the best of my knowledge, *matheracy* was only used previously by the eminent Japanese educator, Tadasu Kawaguchi.

CHAPTER 4. ETHNOMATHEMATICS IN A CHANGING CIVILIZATION

[1] Ubiratan D'Ambrosio: Ética Ecológica. Uma proposta transdisciplinar, *Ecologia Humana, Ética e Educação. A Mensagem de Pierre Danserau*, Paulo Freire Vieira and Maurício Andrés Ribeiro (orgs.), Editora Pallotti/APED, Porto Alegre/Florianópolis, 1999, pp. 639–654.

[2] Ubiratan D'Ambrosio and Marianne Marmé: "*Mathematics, peace and ethics. An introduction*", *Zentralblatt für Didaktik der Mathematik/ZDM*, Jahrgang 30, Juni 1998, Heft 3, pp. 64–66.

[3] See the very provocative the book by Björn Engquist and Wilfried Schmidt (Eds.): *Mathematics Unlimited – 2001 and Beyond*, Springer-Verlag, Berlin, 2001.

[4] Ubiratan D'Ambrosio: "*Diversity, Equity, and Peace: From Dream to Reality*", in *Multicultural and Gender Equity in the Mathematics Classroom. The Gift of Diversity*, 1997 Yearbook of the NCTM/National Council of Teachers of Mathematics, Janet Trentacosta and Margaret J. Kenney, eds., NCTM, Reston, 1997, pp. 243–248.

[5] *Principles and Standards for School Mathematics*, National Council of Teachers of Mathematics, Reston, 2000, pp. 12–14.

[6] Bernard Cassen, Liêm Hoang-Ngoc, Pierre-Andrè Imbert, coords.: *Contre la dictature dês marchés*, ATTAC/La Dispute/Syllepse/VO éditions, Paris, 1999, p. 40.

[7] Keith Devlin: *Goodbye, Descartes: The End of Logic and the Search for a New Cosmology of the Mind*. John Wiley & Sons, New York, 1997; p. 283.

[8] The selective function of mathematics can already be read about in Plato's Republic, and it is taken up again in the proposals for the foundation of the *École Polytéchnique*, in 1800.

[9] The thinking of the eminent sociologist of British education, Basil Bernstein, is synthesized in the book by Ana Maria Domingos, Helena Barradas, Helena Rainha and Isabel Pestana Neves: *A Teoria de Bernstein em Sociologia da Educação*, Fundação Calouste Gulbenkian, Lisboa, 1986.

[10] See the doctoral dissertation by Geraldo Pompeu Jr.: *Bringing Ethnomathematics into the School Curricula: An Investigation of Teachers Attitude and Pupils Learning*, Ph.D. Thesis, Department of Education, University of Cambridge, 1992.

[11] Mariana Kawall Leal Ferreira: *Madikauku. Os Dez Dedos da Mão. Matemática e Povos Indígenas do Brasil*, MEC/SEF, Brasília, 1998.

[12] See the dramatic case in the novel by Louis-Ferdinand Céline: *Viagem ao fim da noite*, translation by Rosa Freire D'Aguiar (orig.1932), Companhia das Letras, São Paulo, 1994, whose scenario is Africa. This is one of the best examples of how mathematics is used by the colonizer to confuse and fool the native population.

[13] Eduardo Sebastiani Ferreira: *Etnomatemática. Uma proposta metodológica*. Série Reflexão em Educação Matemática, vol. 3, Universidade Santa Úrsula, Rio de Janeiro, 1997, p. 43.

[14] Ubiratan D'Ambrosio: *"Mathematics and peace: Our responsibilities"*, Zentralblatt für Didaktik der Mathematik/ZDM, Jahrgang 30, Juni 1998, Heft 3, pp. 67−73.

[15] Ubiratan D'Ambrosio: *A Era da Consciência*, Editora Fundação Peirópolis, São Paulo, 1997.

[16] Ubiratan D'Ambrosio: *"On Environmental mathematics education"*, Zentralblatt für Didaktik der Mathematik/ZDM 94/6, pp. 171−174.

BIBLIOGRAPHY*

Acioly, N.M. *A lógica do jogo do bicho: compreensão ou utilização de regras?* (Mestrado), Recife: Universidade Federal de Pernambuco, Programa de Psicologia Cognitiva, 1985.

Akizuki, Yasuo. "Proposal to I.C.M.I.", *L'Enseignement mathématique*, t.V, fasc. 4, 1960, pp. 288-289.

Albanese, Denise. *New Sience, New World*, Duke University Press, Durham, 1996.

Alberoni, Francesco. *Gênese. Como se criam os mitos, os valores e as instituições da civilização ocidental*, translation by Mario Fondelli, Rocco, Rio de Janeiro, 1991 (orig.ed. 1989).

Almeida, Manoel de Campos. *Origens da Matemática*, Editora Universitária Champagnat, Curitiba, 1998.

Amâncio, Chateaubriand Nunes. *Os Kanhgág da Bacia do Tibagi: Um estudo etnomatemático em comunidades Indígenas*, Masters thesis, Instituto de Geociências e Ciências Exatas, UNESP, Rio Claro, 1999.

Ascher, Márcia and Robert Ascher. *Code of the Quipus: a study in media, mathematics and culture*, The University of Michigan Press, Ann Arbor, 1981.

Bello, Samuel López. *Etnomatemática: relações e tensões entre as distintas formas de explicar e conhecer*, Doctoral dissertation, Faculdade de Educação da UNICAMP, Campinas, 2000.

Bonotto, Cinzia. *"Sull'uso di artefatti culturali nell'insegnamento-apprendimento della matematica/About the use of cultural artifacts in the teaching-learning of mathematics"*, *L'Educazione Matematica*, Anno XX, Serie VI,1(2),1999, pp. 62-95.

Borba, Marcelo de Carvalho. *Um estudo de Etnomatemática: Sua incorporação na elaboração de uma proposta pedagógica para o Núcleo Escola da favela da Vila Nogueira/ São Quirino*, Masters thesis, Instituto de Geociências e Ciências Exatas da UNESP, Rio Claro, 1987.

---

* Only the books and works that appear in the text and notes are included here.

83

Borsato, José Carlos. *Uma experiência de integração curricular: projeto áreas verdes*, Masters dissertation, Ensino de Ciências e Matemática, UNICAMP/OEA/MEC, 1984.

Buriasco, Regina Luzia Corio de. *Matemática de fora e de dentro da escola: do bloqueio à transição*, Masters thesis, Instituto de Geociências e Ciências Exatas da UNESP, Rio Claro, 1989.

Butterworth, Brian. *What Counts. How Every Brain Is Hardwired for Math*, The Free Press, New York, 1999.

Carraher, Terezinha, David Carraher, Analúcia Schliemann. *Na vida dez, na escola zero*, Cortez Editora, São Paulo, 1988.

Cascudo, Luis da Câmara. *História da alimentação no Brasil*, Coleção Brasiliense, São Paulo, 1967.

Cassen, Bernard, Liêm Hoang-Ngoc, Pierre-Andrè Imbert, coords.. *Contre la dictature dês marchés*, ATTAC/La Dispute/Syllepse/VO éditions, Paris, 1999.

Céline, Louis-Ferdinand. *Viagem ao fim da noite*, translation by Rosa Freire D'Aguiar (orig.1932), Companhia das Letras, São Paulo, 1994.

Chouraqui, André. *No Princípio (Gênesis)*, translation by Carlino Azevedo, Imago Editora, Rio de Janeiro, 1995.

Closs, Michael P., ed.. *Native Americans Mathematics*, University of Texas Press, Austin, 1986.

Coménio, J. A. *Didáctica Magna. Tratado da arte universal de ensinar tudo a todos* [orig.edn. 1656], Introdução, Tradução e Notas de Joaquim Ferreira Gomes, Fundação Calouste Gulbenkian, 1966.

Covello, Sergio Carlos. *Comenius. A construção da pedagogia*. Editora Comenius, São Paulo, 1999.

D'Ambrosio, Beatriz Silva. Formação de Professores de Matemática para o Século XXI: o Grande Desafio, *Pro-Posições*, vol.4, n°1[10], março de 1993, p. 35−41.

D'Ambrosio, Ubiratan (org.). *O Ensino de Ciências e Matemática na América Latina*, Editora da UNICAMP/Papirus Editora, Campinas, 1984, pp. 202−203.

D'Ambrosio, Ubiratan and Marianne Marmé. "*Mathematics, peace and ethics*". An introduction, *Zentralblatt für Didaktik der Mathematik/ZDM*, Jahrgang 30, Juni 1998, Heft 3.

D'Ambrosio, Ubiratan. *A era da consciência*, Editora Fundação Peirópolis, São Paulo, 1997.

D'Ambrosio, Ubiratan. "Teoria das catástrofes: Um estudo em sociologia da ciência", *THOT. Uma Publicação Transdisciplinar da Associação Palas Athena*, n.67, 1997, pp. 38−48.

D'Ambrosio, Ubiratan. "*A Historiographical Proposal for Non-western Mathematics*", in Helaine Selin, ed.: *Mathematics Across Cultures. The History of Non-western Mathematics,* Kluwer Academic Publishers, Dordrecht, 2000, pp. 79–92.

D'Ambrosio, Ubiratan. "A matemática na época das grandes navegações e início da colonização", *Revista Brasileira de História da Matemática,* v.1, n.1, 2001.

D'Ambrosio, Ubiratan. "*Diversity, Equity, and Peace: From Dream to Reality*", in *Multicultural and Gender Equity in the Mathematics Classroom. The Gift of Diversity* 1997 Yearbook of the NCTM/National Council of Teachers of Mathematics, Janet Trentacosta and Margaret J. Kenney, eds., NCTM, Reston, 1997, pp. 243–248.

D'Ambrosio, Ubiratan. "*The cultural dynamics of the encounter of two worlds after 1492 as seen in the development of scientific thought*", Impact of science on society, n.167, v.42/3, 1992, pp. 205–214.

D'Ambrosio, Ubiratan. "Ética ecológica. Uma proposta transdisciplinar", in *Ecologia Humana, Ética e Educação. A Mensagem de Pierre Danserau,* Paulo Freire Vieira e Maurício Andrés Ribeiro (orgs.), Editora Pallotti/APED, Porto Alegre/Florianópolis, 1999, p. 639-654.

D'Ambrosio, Ubiratan. *Etnomatemática. Arte ou técnica de explicar e conhecer,* Editora Ática, São Paulo, 1990.

D'Ambrosio, Ubiratan. "*Mathematics and peace: Our resposibilities*", *Zentralblatt für Didaktik der Mathematik/ZDM,* Jahrgang 30, Juni 1998, Heft 3, pp. 67–73.

D'Ambrosio, Ubiratan. "*On Environmental mathematics education*", *Zentralblatt für Didaktik der Mathematik/ZDM,* 94/6, pp. 171–174.

D'Ambrosio, Ubiratan. *Educação para uma sociedade em transição,* Papirus Editora, Campinas, 1999.

Devlin, Keith. *Goodbye, Descartes: The End of Logic and the Search for a New Cosmology of the Mind.* John Wiley & Sons, New York, 1997, p. 283.

Domingos, Ana Maria, Helena Barradas, Helena Rainha e Isabel Pestana Neves. *A Teoria de Bernstein em Sociologia da Educação,* Fundação Calouste Gulbenkian, Lisboa, 1986.

Dreifus, Claudia. "*Do Androids Dream? M.I.T. Is Working on It (A Conversation with Anne Foerst)*", *The New York Times,* November 7, 2000.

Engquist, Björn e Wilfried Schmidt, editors. *Mathematics Unlimited – 2001 and Beyond*, Springer-Verlag, Berlin, 2001.

Eglash, Ron. *African Fractals. Modern Computing and Indigeneous Design*, Rutgers University Press, New Brunswick, 1999.

Eglash, Ron. Anthropological Perspectives on Ethnomathematics, in Selin, Helaine, ed.: *Mathematics Across Cultures. The History of Non-Western Mathematics*, Kluwer Academic Publishers, Dordrecht, 2000, pp. 13–22.

Estrella, Eduardo. *El Pan de América. Etnohistória de los Alimentos Aborígenes en el Ecuador*, Centro de Estúdios Históricos, Madrid, 1986.

Ferreira, Eduardo Sebastiani. *Etnomatemática. Uma proposta metodológica.* Série Reflexão em Educação Matemática, v.3, Universidade Santa Úrsula, Rio de Janeiro, 1997.

Ferreira, Mariana Kawall Leal. *Madikauku. Os Dez Dedos da Mão. Matemática e Povos Indígenas do Brasil,* MEC/SEF, Brasília, 1998.

Flandrin, Jean-Louis e Massimo Montanari (orgs.). *História da alimentação*, translation by Luciano Vieira Machado and Guilherme João de Freitas Teixeira, 2ª edição, Estação Liberdade, São Paulo, 1998 (orig. ed. 1996).

Frankenstein, Marilyn. *Relearning Mathematics. A Different Third R – Radical Mathematics*, Free Association Books, London, 1989.

Gerbi, Antonello. *O novo mundo. História de uma polêmica (1750–1900),* translation by Bernardo Joffily (orig. 1996), Companhia das Letras, São Paulo, 1996.

Gerdes, Paulus. *Sobre o despertar do Pensamento geométrico*, Editora da UFPR, Curitiba, 1992.

Gopnik, Alison, Andrew N. Meltzoff & Patrícia K. Kuhl. *The Scientist in the Crib. Minds, Brains, and How Children Learn*, William Morrow and Company, Inc., New York, 1999.

Herôdotos. *História*, translation by Mário da Gama Kury, Editora Universidade de Brasília, Brasília, 1985, p. 121.

Humboldt, Alexander von. *Cosmos. A Sketch of the Physical Description of the Universe*, 2 vols., tr. E.C. Otté (1858; orig. 1845–1862), The Johns Hopkins University Press, Baltimore, 1997.

Knijnik, Gelsa. *Exclusão e resistência. Educação matemática e legitimidade cultural*, Artes Médicas, Porto Alegre, 1996.

Lakatos, Imre and Paul Feyerabend. *For and Against Method: Including Lakato's Lectures on Scientific Method and the Lakatos-Feyerabend Correspondence.* Edited and with an introduction by Matteo Motterlini, The University of Chicago Press, Chicago, 1999.

Malba Tahan. *O jogo do bicho à luz da matemática*, Grafipar Editora, Curitiba, s/d [after 1975].

Manacorda, Mario Alighiero. *História da educação. Da antiguidade aos nossos dias*, translation by Gaetano Lo Monaco, Cortez Editora, São Paulo, 1996.

Marafon, Adriana César de Mattos. *A influência da família na aprendizagem da matemática*, Masters thesis, Instituto de Geociências e Ciências Exatas da UNESP, Rio Claro, 1996.

Marcale, Jean. *La grande déesse: Mythes et sanctuaires*, Editions Albin Michel, Paris, 1997.

Maturana Romesin, Humberto. *"The Effectiveness of Mathematical Formalisms"*, Cybernetics & Human Knowing, v. 7, n. 2-3, 2000, pp. 147–150.

McNeill, William H. *"Passing Strange: The Convergence of Evolutionary Science with Scientific History"*, History and Theory, v. 40, n.1, February 2001, pp. 1–15.

Monteiro, Alexandrina. *Etnomatemática: as possibilidades pedagógicas num curso de alfabetização para trabalhadores rurais assentados*, Doctoral dissertation, Faculdade de Educação da UNICAMP, Campinas, 1998.

Neeleman, Wilhelm. *Ensino de Matemática em Moçambique e sua relação com a cultura tradicional*, Masters thesis, Instituto de Geociências e Ciências Exatas da UNESP, 1993.

Nobre, Sergio R. *Aspectos sociais e culturais no desenho curricular da matemática*, Masters thesis, Instituto de Geociências e Ciências Exatas da UNESP, Rio Claro, 1989.

Oliveras, Maria Luisa. *Etnomatemáticas en Trabajos de Artesania Andaluza. Su Integración en un Modelo para la Formación de Profesores y en la Innovación del Currículo Matemático Escolar*, Doctoral dissertation, Universidad de Granada, Espanha, 1995.

Oliveras, Maria Luisa. *Etnomatemáticas. Formación de profesores e innovación curricular*, Editorial Comares, Granada, 1996.

Pekonen, Osmo. *"Gerbert of Aurillac: Mathematician and Pope"*, The Mathematical Intelligencer, v. 22, n. 4, 2000, pp. 67–70.

Pompeu Jr., Geraldo. *Bringing Ethnomathematics into the School Curricula: Na Investigation of Teachers Attitude and Pupils Learning*, Ph.D. Thesis, Department of Education, University of Cambridge, 1992.

Povinelli, Daniel J. *Folk Physics for Apes. The Chimpanzee's Theory of How the World Works*, Oxford University Press, Oxford, 2000.

Powell, Arthur B. and Marilyn Frankenstein. eds.: *Ethnomathematics. Challenging Eurocentrism in Mathematics Education*, SUNY Press, Albany, 1997.

Principles and Standards for School Mathematics, National Council of Teachers of Mathematics, Reston, 2000.

Rabiela, Teresa Rojas and William T. Sanders. *Historia de la agricultura. Época prehispanica – siglo XVI*, Instituto Nacional de Antropologia e Historia, México, 1985.

Ralston, Anthony. *"Let's Abolish Pencil-and-Paper Arithmetic"*, *Journal of Computers in Mathematics and Science Teaching*, v. 18, n. 2, 1999, pp. 173–194.

Richards, E. G. *Mapping Time. The Calendar and Its History*, Oxford University Press, Oxford, 1998.

Sacks, Oliver. *Um antropólogo em Marte. Sete histórias paradoxais*, translation byBernardo Carvalho, Companhia das Letras, São Paulo, 1995.

Salvador, Frei Vicente do. *História do Brasil 1500–1627*, Revista por Capistrano de Abreu, Rodolfo Garcia e Frei Venâncio Willeke, OFM, Edições Melhoramentos, São Paulo, 1965.

Selin, Helaine. ed.. *Mathematics Across Cultures. The History of Non-Western Mathematics*, Kluwer Academic Publishers, Dordrecht, 2000.

Shockey, Tod L. *The Mathematical Behavior of a Group of Thoracic Cardiovascular Surgeons*, Ph.D. Dissertation, Curry School of Education, University of Virginia, Charlottsville, USA, 1999.

Spengler, Oswald. *A decadência do ocidente. Esboço de uma morfologia da História Universal*, condensed adition by Helmut Werner, translation by Herbert Caro (orig.1959), Zahar Editores, Rio de Janeiro, 1973.

Stevens, Anthony C., Janet M. Sharp, and Becky Nelson. *"The Intersection of Two Unlikely Worlds: Ratios and Drums"*, *Teaching Children Mathematics* (NCTM), v.7, n.6, February 2001, pp. 376–383.

Vergani, Teresa. Teresa Vergani. *Educação Etnomatemática: O que é?*, Pandora Edições, Lisboa, 2000.

Villa, Maria do Carmo. *Conceptions manifestées par les élèves dans une épreuve de simulation d'une situation aléatoire réalisée au moyen d'um matériel concret*, Tèse de Doctorat, Faculte des Sciences de l'Université Laval, Québec, Canada, 1993.

Weng, Juyang, James McClelland, Alex Pentland, Olaf Sporns, Ida Stockman, Mriganka Sur, Esther Thelen. *"Autonomous Mental*

Development by Robots and Machines", *Science*, v. 291, 26 January 2001, pp. 599–600.

Zaslavsky, Claudia. *Africa Counts. Number and Pattern in African Cultures*, Third Edition, Lawrence Hill Books, Chicago, 1999.

Films/Videos

La Guerre du feu dir. Jean-Jacques Annaud, 1982.

Atlântico Negro – Na Rota dos Orixás, dir. Renato Barbieri, Itaú Cultural e Videografia, 1998.

American Beauty, dir. Sam Mendes, 1999.

Gunga Din, dir. George Stevens, 1939.

Kids, dir. Cary Woods, 1995.

Matrix [*The Matrix*], dir. Andy and Larry Wachovsky, 1999.

Blade Runner, dir. Ridley Scott.1991 [orig.1982]

O Homem que Virou Suco, dir. João Batista de Andrade, 1981.

Internet Sites

http://sites.uol.com.br/vello/ubi.htm

http://www.rpi.edu/~eglash/isgem.htm

http://chronicle.com/colloquy/2000/ethnomath/ethnomath.htm

http://www.fe.unb.br/etnomatematica